Saved in Time

Saved in Time

The Fight to Establish Florissant Fossil Beds National Monument, Colorado

ESTELLA B. LEOPOLD AND HERBERT W. MEYER

UNIVERSITY OF NEW MEXICO PRESS

Albuquerque

© 2012 by the University of New Mexico Press
All rights reserved. Published 2012
Printed in the United States of America
17 16 15 14 13 12   1 2 3 4 5 6

LIBRARY OF CONGRESS CATALOGING-IN-PUBLICATION DATA

Leopold, Estella B.
Saved in time : the fight to establish Florissant Fossil Beds National Monument,
Colorado / Estella B. Leopold and Herbert W. Meyer.
p. cm.
Includes bibliographical references and index.
ISBN 978-0-8263-5236-1 (pbk. : alk. paper) — ISBN 978-0-8263-5237-8 (electronic)
1. Florissant Fossil Beds National Monument (Colo.)—History. 2. Defenders of
Florissant, Inc. 3. Fossils—Colorado—Florissant Region—History. 4. Nature con-
servation—Colorado—Florissant Region—History. 5. Environmental protection—
Colorado—Florissant Region—History. I. Meyer, Herbert W. (Herbert William),
1954– II. Title.
QE747.C6L46 2012
333.78'30978858—dc23
2012019472

BOOK DESIGN
Text designed and composed by Catherine Leonardo
in 10.25/13.5 Minion Pro Regular
Display type is Minion Pro

The Bullitt Foundation kindly matched a contribution from Estella Leopold.

We dedicate this book to the many persons and organizations
involved with the popular movement to save the fossil beds
at Florissant and create the national monument

Contents

Illustrations

FIGURES

TABLES

Preface

THIS BOOK RECOUNTS THE ESTABLISHMENT AND SIGNIFICANCE OF A national monument at the world-famous Florissant fossil beds in Colorado. Collaborating on this book are Estella B. Leopold, botanist and professor emeritus at the University of Washington, and Herbert W. Meyer, resident paleontologist at the Florissant Fossil Beds National Monument. Together, we reveal the many stories of this unique and wonderful place. At the heart of the book is the history behind the lively, yet little-known, political battle that led to the monument's foundation in 1969, which Leopold recounts in chapters 2 through 5. As prologue to the preservation story, in chapter 1 Meyer summarizes the early exploration history of Florissant and recounts the sometimes constructive, sometimes destructive endeavors of early fossil collectors and landowners. In chapter 6 Meyer brings the story of the national monument up to date, and in the appendix he describes the kinds of fossils found at Florissant and their significance to paleontology. In chapter 7 Leopold collaborates with writer John Stansfield to ponder the ultimate significance of the fossil beds for posterity and the impact of the monument's creation on environmental law. Throughout the book, we rely on media, legal, and legislative documents from the period of the Florissant campaign, historic papers and scientific data, and the recollections of those of us involved in the fight to save Florissant.

In August 2009, many of the fossil beds activists came together to celebrate the establishment of the Florissant Fossil Beds National Monument and to share with the public the story of the turbulent events of 1969. Though it has been more than four decades since the battle for Florissant began, the experience still burns bright in these stories. We hope readers will get a sense of the civic spirit of the public, of the scientists, of the able attorneys, and of government leaders at all levels, supported by the media, who, in the nick of time, preserved the fossil beds for the exploration and enlightenment of future generations.

Estella B. Leopold and Herbert W. Meyer

Acknowledgments

❦

MANY CONTRIBUTORS PLAYED IMPORTANT ROLES IN THE PREPARATION of this book between 2008 and 2012. Writer John Stansfield worked with us in the early stages of the book, did much of the early editing, and collaborated with Estella Leopold to pen chapter 7. In particular, the authors owe a great debt of gratitude to Jonathan Cobb, who provided extensive comments on the structure and revision of the manuscript. Their assistance went a long way to make the book coherent and readable. We thank W. Clark Whitehorn and the entire editorial staff of the University of New Mexico Press for all aspects of the book's production. Thanks go to Lynn Bahrych, who urged Estella Leopold to write the Florissant story, and her early reviews were helpful.

The National Park Service fully supported Herb Meyer's role as one of the authors. Various individuals provided support for the completion of this book on behalf of the National Park Service. Lindsay Walker, a paleontology intern at Florissant Fossil Beds National Monument sponsored by the Geological Society of America's GeoCorps Program, worked with us extensively during the final preparation of the book, drafting figures, organizing permission requests, photographing landscapes and fossils for several new figures, and providing helpful review comments for the entire manuscript. Conni O'Connor and Christina Whitmore, student employees in paleontology at the monument, worked exhaustively to carefully locate and inventory archival documents and review and format the manuscript. Tim Schad and Butch Street provided information about visitor use statistics, and James Crocket shared his knowledge about the long history of planning for a national monument visitor center at Florissant. Monument superintendent Keith Payne provided a constructive review of the first draft of the entire manuscript, and he painstakingly succeeded in pursuing the construction of a new visitor center, which enabled us to rewrite a happy ending for that section of the book. The National Park Service, through the Rocky Mountain Cooperative Ecosystems Studies Units program, administered by Kathy Tonnessen, provided financial support for this project to Estella Leopold and the University of Washington.

At the University of Washington, thanks are due for the excellent organizational assistance and impressive talent with graphics provided by Stephanie Zaborac-Reed and Jordan Holley. We thank Rebecca Gamboa for tracking down permissions for use of published material. In 2011, the Burke Museum provided helpful publicity for this book.

Beth Simmons of Metro State College in Denver assisted in locating historical information about Charlotte Hill. John A. C. Wright and Chase Davies assisted us in finding the correct versions of photographs. Jack Loeffler of Santa Fe, New Mexico; Victor John Yannacone, jr., of New York; and Roger Hansen of Aurora, Colorado, provided helpful reviews of the text.

Many wonderful people helped the Defenders of Florissant win the battle for Florissant Fossil Beds National Monument in the 1960s. First and foremost were the legal team and key players, including Victor Yannacone, Richard Lamm, Tom Lamm, and Roger Hansen. Bettie Willard's leadership and contributions to the Florissant story are bountiful. For inspiration on the value the fossil beds, much is owed to paleobotanist Harry D. MacGinitie, whom the authors greatly admired. Colorado congressmen and senators, including Representative Frank Evans, Representative Don Brotzman, Representative Byron Rogers, Senator Gordon Allott, and Senator Peter Dominick, carried the torch in Washington.

In Denver, Amy Roosevelt was helpful with tutorials on editing news releases. Most critical in keeping the public aware of developments were Cal Raines for local TV coverage and various Colorado radio stations for excellent support.

Home team support in Colorado was provided by Sandy Cooper, who worked with Bettie Willard at the Thorne Ecological Institute in Boulder, and Elena Slusser, secretary at the Colorado Open Space Coordinating Council office in Denver. Grateful thanks also go to the brave crew who helped locate the developer's bulldozers, including leader Vim Crane Wright, along with Carolyn Johnson, Hollie Buchan, "Didda" Buchan, and Mary Burton. Many folks assisted the Colorado Open Space Coordinating Council and wrote to their members of Congress and/or testified in the Senate hearing, including Ruth and Bob Weiner, Karen Porter, Kay Collins, Susan Marsh, Hugh Kingery, Rick and Dorie Bradley, Bill Bradley, Dick Beidleman, Larry Crowley, Karen Hillhouse, Nancy Swank, Roger Sanborn's Boys Camp, Thea Phinney, Harry Swift, Charles Agerholm, Elaine Appell, and untold more. Special thanks to Ed Connors and the other Coloradans who helped us raise funding for the project. Clancey Gordon suggested court action. Archaeologist Joe Ben Wheat from the University of Colorado at Boulder helped Bettie Willard and Estella Leopold write the first draft of the brief that the lawyers used in court. Sally Story and colleagues at the Denver Art Museum, and Jim West and Don Bower at *Colorado Magazine* helped spread the word for events.

Individuals or groups outside of Colorado that helped the Defenders of Florissant seek funding include Dillon Ripley at the Smithsonian Institute; Richard Pough at the American Museum of Natural History; A. Starker Leopold at the University of California, Berkeley; Joe Hickey at the University of Wisconsin, Madison; and Art Cridland at Washington State University, Pullman. In Washington, D.C., Wendy Sasaki, at the Bureau of the Budget, provided statistics, while Representative Henry Reuss, Democrat from Wisconsin, and Russ Train, undersecretary of the U.S. Department of the Interior, gave us useful advice when needed.

Numerous writers, such as Luther Carter and Philip Boffey of *Science*, spread the message about Florissant nationally. Publications that also assisted the Defenders of Florissant in reaching the American public include the *New Yorker*, *New York Times*, *Rocky Mountain News*, *Denver Post*, *Colorado Springs Gazette*, *Sierra Club Bulletin*, *Trail & Timberline*, *Mines Magazine*, *Washington Post*, *Gems and Minerals Magazine*, and *Christian Science Monitor*.

Gratitude is due to many clubs and nonprofit organizations in Colorado, Washington, D.C., and elsewhere that directly participated in the effort to preserve the fossil beds: Aiken Ornithological Society, American Camping Association, Association for Beautiful Colorado Roads, Colorado Federation of Garden Clubs, Colorado Federation of Women's Clubs, Colorado Hawking Club, Colorado Mineral Society, Colorado Mountain Club, Colorado Open Space Coordinating Council, Colorado Wildlife Federation, Colorado

Whitewater Association, Denver Audubon Society, Denver Botany Club, Denver Field Ornithologists, El Paso PARC Committee, General Federation of Women's Clubs (Washington, D.C), Girl Scouts of Denver, Colorado, Interprofessional Committee on Environmental Design, Izaak Walton League (Colorado Springs, Colorado), Izaak Walton League (Laramie, Wyoming), League of Women Voters (Colorado Springs, Colorado), Mountain Area Planning Council, Men's Gardens Clubs of America, Metropolitan Wildlife Federation, Nature Conservancy (Boulder, Colorado), Plains Conservation Center, PLAN Boulder, Planned Parenthood of Colorado, Regional Parks Association, Rocky Mountain Association of Geologists, Sierra Club (Rocky Mountain chapter), Springs Area Beautiful Association, Trout Unlimited (Cutthroat chapter), Wyoming Audubon Society, and Young Democrats of Colorado.

Last but not least, individuals from the following institutions across the nation offered advice and support to the Florissant campaign: Academy of Natural Sciences (Ruth Patrick, Philadelphia, Pennsylvania); American Conservation Association (George Lamb, staff for Lawrence Rockefeller, New York City); American Museum of Natural History (Nat Colbert and other paleontologists); *Colorado Magazine* (Merl Hastings, publisher); Colorado Springs Chamber of Commerce; Commissioners of Teller County, Colorado; El Pomar Foundation (William T. Tutt, president, Colorado Springs, Colorado); Field Museum of Natural History (Chicago, Illinois); U.S. Department of the Interior (Assistant Secretary Stanley Cain, Deputy Assistant Secretary Charles Caruthers, Staff Assistant Jim Meyers, Dr. Leslie Glasgow, Floyd Gibbons); Los Angeles County Museum; Missouri Botanical Gardens (Peter Raven, St. Louis, Missouri); National Education Association (John M. Lumley); National Park Service Planning Office (Ed Hummel, associate director of planning and transfer, and Adele Wilson, Washington, D.C.); National Geographic Society of New York (Cal Heusser); the Nature Conservancy (Huey Johnson, regional director); New Jersey Academy of Science (Rutgers University); U.S. Senate (Charles Cook, minority counsel); Smithsonian Institution (Serge Mamay); and Waynesburg College (Paul R. Stewart, Waynesburg, Pennsylvania).

Introduction

❦

IN THE SUMMER OF 1969, THE FEDERAL DISTRICT COURT OF DENVER, Colorado, heard arguments in one of the nation's first explicitly environmental cases, that of the Defenders of Florissant, Inc., versus real estate interests that were intent on turning land containing an extraordinary set of ancient fossils into a housing development. For the Florissant Defenders, the case rode a ground swell of public support from an unlikely coalition of people—including conservationists, scientists, outdoor enthusiasts, and local ranchers—whose voices were echoed and re-echoed by the press.

Hanging in the balance that summer was whether the courts would or could successfully protect for future generations the remarkable Florissant fossil beds, replete with unique plant and insect fossils delicately preserved over millions of years. Their disturbance would be a loss forever. Today, there is hardly a paleontologist in the world who has not heard of the fossil beds at Florissant. And because of the site's ultimate preservation, many have been able to see these marvels firsthand, as have hundreds of thousands of visitors from all walks of life. The story of Florissant—the extraordinary richness of its deposits, what they tell us of life's history, and how they were saved—is the subject of this book (figure 0.1).

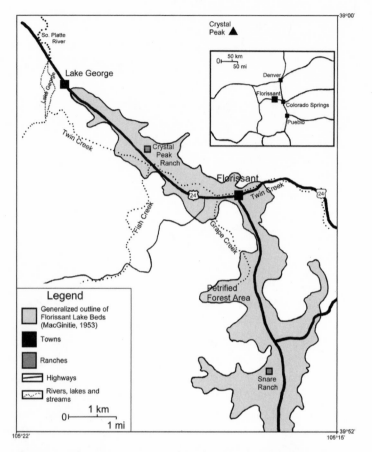

Figure 0.1. The main area covered by the Florissant lake beds (the deposits actually extend 2.5 miles farther south). The lake beds rest on Pikes Peak Granite, which underlies the local area. The valley is thirty miles west of Colorado Springs on U.S. Highway 24. (Drafted by Stephanie Zaborac-Reed.)

Miocene Pompeii

In 1908 a University of Colorado scientist described the Florissant area as a "Miocene Pompeii." Miocene refers to the geologic epoch once thought to include the age of the Florissant beds. Florissant is comparable to Pompeii because ash from volcanic eruptions had preserved the biological organisms of the Florissant region at a moment in time more than 30 million years ago, just as Mount Vesuvius's eruption had frozen the ancient civilization of Italy's Pompeii at a point in time almost 2,000 years ago. Just as a visit to

Pompeii today gives people a glimpse of Roman culture as it was centuries ago, so a Florissant visit enables everyone to see the array of life as it existed there at a moment in time some 34 million years ago.

The impending destruction of such a treasure—a treasure that had remained unharmed for millions of years—for the sake of a land developer's profits and a few new houses moved Victor Yannacone, the talented and colorful legal defender of Florissant. He declared in court that summer of 1969 that to allow the building of summer homes on fossils like these is like using the Dead Sea Scrolls to wrap fish.[1]

Long before the landmark struggles of the 1960s to save Florissant that this book recounts, the significance of the Florissant area was recognized. The first Americans to revere this place were probably people of the Ute tribe, who had lived and hunted in the region for many generations. But it was not until the 1870s that scientists of the federal government's Hayden Survey described the geology of Florissant's rich beds and sent samples of beautifully preserved fossils back east. There, paleontologists Leo Lesquereux and Samuel Scudder developed a series of reports on the fossils that inspired a succession of paleontologists—a "Who's Who" of science—to journey to Florissant in the ensuing decades. Their work paid homage to the valley's plants and animals of stone.

The time period spanned by the Florissant fossil beds—36 to 34 million years ago—falls not within the younger Miocene epoch as once thought, but in the Eocene epoch, which lasted from 56 million to 34 million years ago. During most of the Eocene, the climate of the Northern Hemisphere was typically tropical and amazingly warm from low latitudes to high. Following the end of the Eocene, the climate began to cool and vegetation started to change. Much of Florissant's significance comes from what it tells us about this period of change. Some of the plants that grew at Florissant then were similar to those found far to the south today in places such as Mexico, and even as far away as East Asia.[2]

Landscapes Then and Now

What was the world like 34 million years ago? A remarkable aspect of Florissant is what we can learn from what survives there. Enter the Florissant valley by traveling west from Colorado Springs and look around when you arrive. The landscape of the basin itself, scientists have determined, is much the same in outline as it was 34 million years ago. But life was different then. The plants and animals that have turned to stone silently tell us of an ancestral life—a golden age of huge redwoods (now unknown in Colorado), broad-leaved trees, plovers, spiders, and fish quite different from today's.

If you climb Crystal Peak to the north of the Florissant basin, on the eastern horizon you can see Pikes Peak about fourteen miles away (plate 1). Below, at an elevation 8,200 feet (2,500 meters) above sea level, you can see the ten-mile-long grassy meadows that outline the contours of what 34 million years ago was Lake Florissant. "It will appear that this elevated lake must have been a beautiful, though shallow, sheet of water," Samuel Scudder surmised in 1881, based on the character of the fish fossilized and the sun-cracked shales found within its perimeter.[3] "Topaz Butte [now known as Crystal Peak] . . . guarded the head of the lake . . . rising three or four hundred meters above its level. It was hemmed in on all sides by nearer granitic hills, whose wooded slopes came to the water's edge."

Along the southwestern flanks of the lake can be found the petrified remains of the famous redwood trees, huge upright trunks still standing as they grew, 16 to 20 feet (5 or 6 meters) high and up to 13 feet (4 meters) thick. Above the valley bottom today is a ponderosa pine and sagebrush woodland, but 34 million years ago this terrain was a warm temperate zone, with pine, many broad-leaved trees, occasional palm trees, abundant termites, and a great variety of insects and ferns. The terrain must have included shallow waters and wetlands where numerous cattails grew, as these are obvious in the laminated sediments.

If we stand among the silicified stumps near the U.S. National Park Service (NPS) office and look east, we can imagine the mountain slopes near Pikes Peak cloaked in conifer woodland much as they are today, but mixed with species now either everywhere extinct or at least gone from Colorado. The earliest known relatives of ponderosa pine and mountain mahogany can be found here, but along with them, too, were evergreen holly-leaved oaks and the now-Asian golden-rain trees. The higher and cooler slopes held extinct species of true fir, and spruce. On the balds, the hottest slopes, scrub greasewood, grasses, and small shrubs of evening primrose grew. Most novel were the rich riverine forests by the lake that were dominated by redwoods towering probably more than 200 feet (60 meters) high, mixed with broad-leaved trees of the walnut, birch, beech, and elm families.

If one of the pleasures in visiting Florissant is seeing the landscapes (figure 0.2) and imagining what they were like in outline 34 million years ago, what makes the experience so vivid is the incredible preservation of the

Figure 0.2. Landscape of the Florissant valley looking north toward Crystal Peak. The conifers are mainly ponderosa pine on top of the old lake bed area. (Photograph by Lindsay Walker; courtesy of Florissant Fossil Beds National Monument.)

fossil-bearing rocks themselves. It is a far different experience than looking at a set of hand-sized fossils on display in a glass cabinet.

The condition of many of the fossils is outstanding. The blanket of fine-grained volcanic ash that entombed the plants and insects often preserved even the most delicate insect wings and antennae, fish scales, and flower petals. The excellent preservation of the organisms at Florissant has permitted scientists to identify more than seventeen hundred species of organisms there, making it one of the richest fossil sites in the world. The diversity of the insect fauna in itself is daunting. Samuel Scudder alone identified some six hundred insect species, including a wide range of spiders, bees, ants, butterflies, beetles, mayflies, hornets, wasps, sawflies, leaf rollers, rove beetles, midges, and termites. In 1881 he wrote enthusiastically of his Florissant finds: "[This] single locality . . . yielded in a single summer more than double the number of specimens which the famous localities at Oeningen, in Bavaria, furnished [paleobotanist Oswald] Heer in thirty years."[4] These insect and plant finds are but a small sample of the truly amazing diversity of Florissant's fossil record. The fauna identified, for example, includes many fishes, small aquatic biota, and a few mammals such as the huge brontothere and a primitive horse.

The huge number and diversity of fossils have allowed scientists to construct a picture of what the Florissant ecosystem once was like with its unique assemblage of plant and animal species. Today, some Florissant genera grow only in Southeast Asia, some only in California and Mexico, and some have gone extinct. But once they were together at Florissant.

Another wonder of Florissant is the opportunity it gives visitors to "travel back in time" and contrast species of the past with those of today, and to see how similar yet different they could be. Charles Darwin was inspired to his loftiest theory in Brazil while standing at a fossil bed where relatively small, modern capybara rodents roamed over the fossilized remains of huge capybaras of the past. "Could it be they are actually related, the one with the other?" he might have asked, "And if so, how?" Similarly intriguing questions can also be asked at Florissant.

In Lake Florissant, age-old algae grew, just as they did 300 million years before in the Pennsylvanian period, and just as they do today, only the ostracodes and species of fish that once preyed on them are now defunct. Part of the story Florissant illustrates so well is that life of the past mixed something old with something new and was ever changing. Ancient algae and horsetails helped support a younger Florissant ecosystem that was rapidly evolving, with new models of fishes, mammals, specialized insects, and flowers appearing. Though the individual specimens we see at Florissant are captured in stone at a moment in time, the species of which they were a part were anything but fixed in their evolution.

These are the glories that were. The paper shales—the paper-thin ash layers—of Lake Florissant open to show us an archival record kept in no other library. This place is unique in time and space. As Harry D. MacGinitie of the University of California at Berkeley told the U.S. senators at a public hearing in Colorado in 1969, "The land occupied by the lake beds is not of particularly great value . . . but as a page of earth history from the dim past it is priceless."[5]

Florissant Under Siege

By the mid-1960s, this remarkable formation of nature in the Florissant valley, this unique page of Earth history, was at risk for an extinction of its own. A growing human population had made central Colorado an increasingly desirable place to live, and real estate interests saw a chance to cash in on homeowner desires. When the Park Service announced in 1964 that the area would be proposed as a national monument—a status that would protect the land from development—the risk to Florissant ironically accelerated, as real estate developers quickly attempted to buy up the increasingly desirable land from local ranchers. A-frame housing was sprouting up, and developers were buying up land along the margins of the proposed monument.

The logic of the developers was simple: the more of the core area they were able to start bulldozing and building on, the less attractive would be the idea of a national monument there, and should a monument be declared, the surrounding land was likely to increase in value. This was all taking place some years before the first Earth Day, celebrated in 1970, which marked the ground swell of national environmental concern. It also came before implementation of the 1969 National Environmental Policy Act (NEPA) and requirements for environmental impact reports.

At first, saving the Florissant fossil beds and their unique and irreplaceable plant and insect fossils was a priority for only a few stalwart and determined Coloradans and their supporters. These supporters included not only Colorado conservationists but also scientists who recognized the extraordinary importance of the Florissant fossils, and perhaps surprisingly, some of the local ranchers whose land included the spectacular fossil *Sequoia* stumps. Without recourse to the environmental legislation that would only later be passed, such concerned citizens at the local and state level in the 1960s were often pretty much on their own in fighting conservation battles.

In 1964, my friend Beatrice Willard, a member of the state's Sierra Club chapter, and I (then active in the Colorado Mountain Club) began to lead field trips to the Florissant valley to acquaint a wider public with the extraordinary natural treasures there. We were inspired in that year by the introduction in the U.S. Congress of draft legislation to protect the area. We hoped that more public support for the National Park Service's efforts to preserve the Florissant area would forestall further development before it was too late. Others in the two outdoor clubs soon began to help by also leading field trips to Florissant. On some of these visits we invited members of the press along so they could develop a close-up understanding of Florissant's wonders.

Fortunately, at about this time, local conservationists and outdoor enthusiasts had come to recognize that an umbrella organization for Colorado's outdoor clubs would make it possible for everyone to work together more efficiently and wield more political power. One of the first initiatives of the resulting umbrella group, the Colorado Open Space Coordinating Council (COSCC), was to help promote monument status for Florissant.

The efforts to save Florissant and preserve it for future generations were essentially twofold in nature: first, building the citizens' movement and education campaign designed to put pressure on Congress to grant monument status to Florissant without delay; and second, introduction of legal moves to block further real estate development in the area so that everything possible of substance that could be preserved at the site would be.

When the citizens' groups took the real estate developers to court, they sought a restraining order to keep the bulldozers from rolling over the fossil beds to dig roads for housing developments. The case of *Defenders of Florissant, Inc. v. Park Land Company* was brought in the Federal District Court of Denver by some of the country's pioneering environmental lawyers, including New Yorker Victor Yannacone, Richard Lamm (later governor of Colorado), and Roger Hansen, founder of COSCC. In his pleadings to the court, Yannacone captured in another memorable line something of the spirit of the dispute when he said that using the Florissant fossils for real estate development is like using the Rosetta Stone for grinding corn.

Yannacone dramatically delineated essential dimensions of the Florissant case, particularly why ethical care of the land is a necessity and why the fossils of the Florissant area were of such great importance that they should belong to the people of the United States for safekeeping. The fact that the citizens' groups were ultimately successful in their efforts set an example for how the citizenry could fight against property rights that would demean and disturb special lands and for the ethical care of such lands that would preserve their educational, recreational, and aesthetic value.

The Florissant fight was an early test case of what could be accomplished. It was followed by many environmental successes in the Rocky Mountain region and was an important step toward the many fine environmental laws of the 1970s, which have helped to protect the environments of the United States. It was, in effect, the first national environmental victory brought through the courts.

By making Florissant a national monument in 1969, the United States guaranteed protection to an important natural place, a quiet place where we can think about our earthly roots. Looking up, we can watch the kestrels dive like blue angels in search of grasshoppers, while we stand in the graveyard of a great fallen community—the Florissant ecosystem of the Eocene. Here, with the wonder of a child, we can take the mental journey back through the geologic ages. The experience gives us the perspective of time and evolution—from those birds that were and now lie encased in ash, to these birds that are and now fly overhead. By touching those stones we may feel the same wonder that may have inspired members of the Ute tribe. We can imagine our own version of dynamic life and feel the pulse of the restless Earth. And we are able to have this experience because the battle to save the Florissant fossil beds succeeded (figure 0.3).

Estella B. Leopold

Figure 0.3. The petrified "Redwood Trio" of *Sequoia* with two young admirers. (Photograph by Estella B. Leopold.)

Chapter One

Unearthing Wonders

🌿

HERBERT W. MEYER

SINCE THE 1870S, MANY PALEONTOLOGISTS, FOSSIL COLLECTORS, SETTLERS, entrepreneurs, and tourist operators have shaped careers from their fossil discoveries at Florissant.[1] In 1871, Theodore Meade, a young butterfly-collecting college student from Cornell University, gathered some of the first fossils from Florissant to end up in the hands of scientists. The following year, one of the area's settlers, James Costello, who would meet and host some of the early scientific visitors to the region, established a post office and named the town after his native Florissant, Missouri. As news of the fossil finds spread and scientific parties began to arrive, Florissant quickly became known as one of the first significant fossil sites of the American West. The timing couldn't have been better. It was a critical period for the rapidly developing science of paleontology, coming as it did less than twenty years after Charles Darwin published *Origin of Species*, in which he presented the new idea that life was driven by evolution. Fossils were the key to understanding the details of this process.

Early European collectors had shown that fossil shells in the rock changed in successively higher strata, implying that this change represented a time sequence. In the early 1880s, the French scientists Alexandre Brongniart and Georges Cuvier used fossils to determine the order of rock strata by developing a kind of "tree of life." By the time of Darwin, the work of the famous English geologist Charles Lyell had established that fossils are

1

unequivocally useful to delineate periods of geologic time. Lyell outlined these major periods in his treatise *Principles of Geology*, a volume that Darwin carried with him on his voyage on the HMS *Beagle*.

Breaking New Scientific Ground

The Hayden Survey of the Great Plains and Rocky Mountains (1867–1878) was the first government-sponsored scientific expedition to take an interest in the valley at Florissant. A geologist with that survey, A. C. Peale, visited Florissant in 1873 and noted the presence of the fossil-rich lake deposits and about twenty or thirty petrified stumps.[2] Three pioneering paleontologists—Leo Lesquereux, Samuel H. Scudder, and Edward Drinker Cope—all went on to describe in the volumes of the Hayden Survey hundreds of new species discovered at Florissant, thereby making them known to the world.

In 1873, Lesquereux (figure 1.1) wrote the first scientific publication to include Florissant, which described its fossil plants.[3] He had moved to America from Switzerland, deaf and at first unable to understand English, but very much at home with nature and science. He supported himself as a watchmaker and thus could work only part time studying the fossil plants that were collected by the government surveys. Nevertheless, he was among the first to unravel the natural history of the ancient forests of the West and became one of the founders of North American paleobotany, the study of fossil plants. We have no evidence to show that he actually visited Florissant, yet many of the Florissant fossils certainly found their way into his hands. He described more than one hundred new species from Florissant alone in two large monographs he published in 1878 and 1883.[4]

The fossil fish found at Florissant were first systematically described by Cope of the Philadelphia Academy of Natural Sciences, also in the mid-1870s.[5] Cope was one of the first vertebrate paleontologists to study fossil bones

Figure 1.1. Leo Lesquereux. (Image from Smithsonian Institution Archives.)

Figure 1.2. Charlotte Hill (A) was an early homesteader at Florissant who collected many important fossils, including the world-famous fossil butterfly *Prodryas persephone* (B). (Photograph from the collection of Florissant Fossil Beds National Monument; specimen MCZ-1, courtesy of the Museum of Comparative Zoology, Harvard University.)

B.

A.

from the West. He was especially interested in the many dinosaurs that were discovered (in the early 1870s) only a few miles south of Florissant at Garden Park, near Canon City, though in rocks much older than those containing the Florissant fossils. These dinosaur discoveries led to the famous "bone wars" between Cope and Othniel Marsh of Yale University, and the two became bitter rivals in their attempts to become the first to describe these dinosaur fossils. Though arguably not as exciting as dinosaurs, fossil fish are among the few vertebrates found at Florissant.

By the mid-1870s, word of the Florissant finds led to two important scientific explorations of the area in the summer of 1877. The first was that of the Princeton Scientific Expedition, a group of eighteen college students, two professors, a proctor, and a janitor. The expedition had been organized by three of the students: Henry Fairfield Osborn, William Berryman Scott, and Francis Speir Jr., all of whom later went on to prominent careers, two of them in paleontology. Traveling by Indian ponies and covered wagons as they explored Wyoming, Utah, and Colorado, the group visited Florissant for two days in mid-July. After meeting one of the local homesteaders, Charlotte Hill (figure 1.2), and seeing the fossils in her collection, they realized they had come upon an important find. They acquired from Hill many of the fossil insects and leaves they brought back, but they excavated some leaf and fish fossils on their own as well. Many of these fossils later became the type specimens used to describe new species.

In mid-August of that year, Massachusetts entomologist Samuel Scudder (figure 1.3) rode into the town of Florissant in the company of one of Colorado's

Figure 1.3. Samuel Scudder. (Image from Archives of the Museum of Comparative Zoology, Ernst Mayr Library, Harvard University.)

early geologists, Arthur Lakes. They were traveling by horseback through central Colorado, collecting live and fossil insects, and were offered a cottage for their stay by James Costello. Like the Princeton students, Scudder and Lakes met with Charlotte and Adam Hill at their homestead and were astonished to see boxes upon boxes of plant and insect fossils in their collection.[6]

With the help of the Hills and Arthur Lakes, Scudder amassed a huge collection by digging a trench on the north side of a mesa, not far from the Hills's house. The trench helped the scientists to uncover and carefully measure the fresh layers of shale, and to split the shale in search of fossils. When exposed to the elements, shale rapidly disintegrates and the fossils it contains are continually lost to natural processes, just like the pages from an ancient, crumbling book.

Scudder and Lakes made some of the first detailed studies of Florissant's geology, and based on these observations, Lakes produced a geologic map of the lake beds, which he completed in watercolor the following winter.[7] Scudder was a pioneer in the study of fossil insects, and in the years that followed, Florissant became a focal point of his distinguished career. The huge variety of new fossils coming from Florissant must have seemed overwhelming at times, yet it gave him unique opportunities to make new discoveries. He made at least two more trips to Florissant and named more species from the site than anyone else ever has. Many of his discoveries were helpful in developing broader ideas about the evolution and distribution of insects through time. Much later Frank Carpenter of Harvard, the most prominent American paleoentomologist of the twentieth century, wrote that it was remarkable how advanced were the fossil insects at Florissant; even at their great age (34 million years), many of them could easily be recognized according to which modern family they belong and even which genus they represent.[8]

The magnitude of Scudder's work can be gauged by his huge 1890 monograph, *The Tertiary Insects of North America*, which is 734 pages in length and weighs more than seven pounds.[9] In this and several other works, Scudder described six hundred fossil insects from Florissant and included an artist's beautiful drawings of most of them (figure 1.4). He was especially interested in the butterflies, and among the famous fossils he is noted for having described was *Prodryas persephone*, a perfect nymphalid butterfly (see figure 1.2) whose existence had been brought to his attention by Charlotte Hill. In addition to having worked for the Hayden Survey from 1886 until 1892, Scudder kept up a long association with the Boston Society of Natural History and Harvard University. In 1902, his collections went to the Museum of Comparative Zoology at Harvard, where they remain today.

Early in the twentieth century, T. D. A. Cockerell of the University of Colorado became fascinated with Florissant after reading some of Scudder's

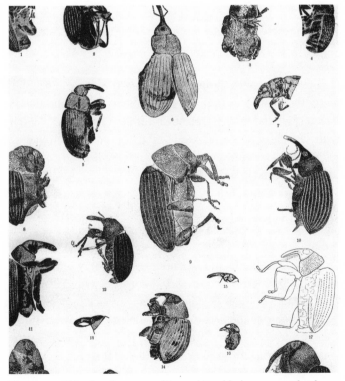

Figure 1.4. This plate from one of Samuel Scudder's monographs shows fine details of the Florissant fossil weevils, which are a type of beetle in the family Curculionidae. (Samuel Scudder, "Tertiary Rhynchophorus Coleoptera of the United States," Monographs of the United States Geological Survey 21 [1893]: plate 6.)

Figure 1.5. T. D. A. Cockerell. (Image from University of Colorado at Boulder Archives, Photolab Collection, Alphabetical Collection, T. D. A. Cockerell.)

work. Joined by a small field party that included his wife (who was to make many remarkable fossil finds of her own) and several other colleagues and students, Cockerell (figure 1.5) organized collecting trips to Florissant between 1906 and 1908. These expeditions were sponsored in part by the American Museum of Natural History, Yale University, and the British Museum, each of which still houses some of his collection.

Cockerell studied not only fossil plants, insects, spiders, and mollusks, but also some of the living bees from the Florissant area. His collection included various butterflies and moths, a giant robber fly, a rare fossil of a moss, and leaves with attached flowering heads of the extinct beech-like *Fagopsis.* Cockerell was especially intrigued by the surprising discovery of a fossil tsetse fly, an insect which today lives only in Africa.

Like Scudder before him, Cockerell was concerned about the loss of Florissant's fossils to amateur collectors and curiosity seekers. "It is very unfortunate that inexperienced collectors throw away many valuable specimens, looking only for conspicuous ones, while from time to time very fine things are preserved by the non-scientific as curiosities and are eventually broken or lost," he commented in 1916. "Many species of Florissant insects are known only by uniques [a single example of a certain species], and in spite of the richness of the field it is impossible to have any assurance that species so represented will ever be found again. . . . To lose or destroy them is like removing a brick from some splendid building; the building will not fall, but the offense is intolerable."[10]

Cockerell's huge collections soon inspired other colleagues to examine Florissant fossils as well. C. T. Brues, for example, described 145 species of Hymenoptera (wasps, ants, bees, and sawflies) and was especially interested in the ichneumons and parasitic wasps, which are insects that lay their eggs in the eggs, larvae, or adults of other insects and often consume their "hosts" during development. In 1909, the famous fossil collector George Sternberg developed a large collection from Florissant that went to the American Museum of Natural History. Three years later, H. F. Wickham, an entomologist from Iowa, collected at Florissant and went on to describe 356 species of beetles new to science.

Frank Carpenter first became interested in fossil insects as a boy, after seeing a picture of the famous Florissant butterfly *Prodryas persephone* (see figure 1.2).[11] In 1920, while still a high school student, he met one of the members of Cockerell's 1906 expedition, the entomologist W. M. Wheeler, at Harvard. The fossil ants from Florissant that Wheeler displayed amazed Carpenter, and he went on to study under Wheeler. In 1992, near the end of his long career at Harvard, Carpenter published two exhaustive volumes on fossil insects for the *Treatise on Invertebrate Paleontology*, in which he listed 765 genera from Florissant.[12]

Harry D. MacGinitie, one of the great paleobotanists of the twentieth century, traveled to Florissant in 1936 and 1937. With the help of a horse-drawn grading blade to remove the soil overburden and a large butcher knife to split the shale, he excavated at three new sites (figure 1.6). He strove to understand all of the plants that made up this ancient vegetation—the whole flora. Beyond simply recognizing and naming the fossil plants, he was interested in broader questions, such as what the ancient climate had been like, how entire communities of plants had changed through time, and where the relatives of Florissant fossil plants lived today. Following service in World War II, MacGinitie published a definitive work on the site, *Fossil Plants of the Florissant Beds, Colorado*, in 1953.[13]

Figure 1.6. Harry D. MacGinitie used a rock hammer and butcher knife to split shale in search of fossils during his 1936–1937 excavations at Florissant. He published the authoritative monograph on the fossil plants in 1953. (Courtesy of Florissant Fossil Beds National Monument.)

"Mac," as he was known, was a mentor and an inspiration for many young scientists, including the two authors of this book, who worked with him during his later years. He also became an articulate advocate for preserving Florissant as a national monument in the 1960s.

These and many other scientists over the decades (table 1.1) have contributed to the study of Florissant's fossils and the complex ancient ecosystem of which the organisms were originally a part. The enormity of this work is one marker of Florissant's significance in the world of paleontology. For more than forty years, Waynesburg College of Pennsylvania even sponsored its summer geology field camp at Florissant, hosting twelve students each session. Inspired by the college's president, Paul R. Stewart, the participants uncovered a large number of fossils during these sessions, and as a result, the school now holds one of the larger collections from Florissant, consisting of about three thousand specimens.

Table 1.1. Significant historical contributors to Florissant paleontology

Paleontologist	Major affiliations during Florissant work	Dates of Florissant publications	Primary contributions at Florissant
L. Lesquereux	Independent; Hayden Survey	1873–1883	First descriptions of fossil plants
S. H. Scudder	Hayden Survey; U.S. Geological Survey; Harvard University Librarian	1876–1900	Described 600 new species of fossil insects
E. D. Cope	Hayden Survey; Academy of Natural Sciences of Philadelphia	1874–1883	Described all species of fossil fish
T. D. A. Cockerell	University of Colorado	1906–1941	Published 130 papers on Florissant and described 333 species of fossil plants, insects, and mollusks
C. T. Brues	Milwaukie Public Museum; Harvard University	1906–1910	Described 145 new species of fossil bees and wasps

H. F. Wickham	University of Iowa; U.S. Bureau of Entomology	1908–1920	Described 356 new species of fossil beetles
F. Carpenter	Harvard University	1930–1992	Described 31 species of fossil ants
A. L. Melander	College of the City of New York; University of California at Riverside	1946–1949	Described 65 species of fossil flies
H. D. MacGinitie	Humboldt State College (California); University of California at Berkeley	1937–1953	Study of fossil plants and the evidence of ancient climate and testified at U.S. Senate hearing in support of creating a national monument

Scientists who came to Florissant over the years removed many fossils—and for good reason. Most fossils, if left in the ground and not collected by paleontologists, have little value when it comes to advancing human knowledge about Earth's past. Twenty or so museums now are known to house Florissant specimens, including natural history museums in New York, Pittsburgh, Berkeley, Cambridge, New Haven, Boulder, Denver, and Chicago, as well as in England and Scotland. Visitors to Florissant sometimes feel that it is tragic that so many of the fossils have left the site, but the fossils scientists took away for study elsewhere have continuing value to scholarship and many are on public display. Fossils carried away by tourists are a different story altogether.

Commerce and Curiosities

At the time the early scientists and tourists arrived in the 1870s, petrified trunks covered the ground in the Florissant valley. Some of the local landowners were already aware of the special scientific and commercial value of their fossil-rich property. In the 1880 census, Adam and Charlotte Hill listed their occupation as specimen collectors, and Charlotte kept a little museum of fossils in her house.[14] Professors from nearby Colorado College who visited the area were able to take anything they wanted, and they began carting off petrified wood by the wagonload. Many other fossils were simply picked up by tourists as curiosities, never to be seen by the scientific world. By the 1890s, Scudder and others were already noticing how rapidly the petrified forest was disappearing. Trees that stood well above the ground were being shortened, and piece by piece, the large stumps grew smaller as the decades passed until, in some cases, nothing remained.

As the Florissant valley was homesteaded, it passed from public to private land and remained so through the 1960s. The owners were legally free in the interim to do as they pleased with their properties. By the time the National Park Service became the custodian of the site in the early 1970s, a century of exploitation had elapsed, and much of the petrified wood was gone, along with thousands of other fossils. But countless leaf and insect fossils were still buried in the shale, and some of the most impressive stumps remained underground where they had been for 34 million years.

As early as 1876, Adam Hill explored the possibility of sending a petrified stump back east for the Centennial International Exhibition in Philadelphia.[15] During the 1880s, scaffolding was built around the "Big Stump" to support the saws being used, unsuccessfully it turned out, to cut it apart so it could more easily be moved. When tracks for the Colorado Midland Railroad were laid to Florissant in 1887, some promoters wanted to load the huge tree—estimated to weigh more than sixty tons—onto the train and send it to the 1893 World's Columbian Exposition in Chicago, but it was too large to move through the narrow railroad tunnels. Because of its gigantic size, another attempt was made to cut it up for transport and display at a major city museum. Rusted saw blades from this failed effort remain even today embedded in the stump where they broke.

Tourists arrived in greater numbers with the coming of the railroad, which made travel to Florissant much easier. The Wildflower Excursion, one of the advertised trains, brought summer tourists into the mountains to see the colorful blooms and the petrified forest (figure 1.7). The visitors collected fossils from an outcrop of shale exposed in one of the railroad cuts on the outskirts of Florissant (figure 1.8), or they bought curiosities from local children, who were ever ready to sell fossils to the tourists when the train came to town. Nobody knows how many fossils went down the mountain on those trains or where they might be today.

Figure 1.7. The "Big Stump" has been one of the most popular tourist attractions at Florissant since the 1880s. This photo shows visitors around 1900. (Courtesy of History Colorado, Buckwalter Collection, scan #20030858.)

Figure 1.8. In the early 1900s, the Colorado Midland Railway operated a special tourist train that came to Florissant from Colorado Springs and allowed passengers the opportunity to stop at this outcrop of Florissant shale to collect fossils. (Courtesy of History Colorado, Buckwalter Collection, scan #20030061.)

With Colorado's continued growth and improved transportation network, more and more people arrived in Florissant. Owners of land containing the fossil beds, eager to capitalize on this influx of visitors, developed two properties as "petrified forests." One of these attractions was located by the Big Stump on land that had belonged to Adam and Charlotte Hill. John Coplen, Charlotte's older brother, and members of the Colorado Museum Association acquired the property in 1883 and leased it for many years. If the purchase was stimulated by the need to protect the area from specimen dealers and curiosity hunters who were taking fossils, the preservation instincts of the new owners only went so far. It was apparently their organization that wanted to cut the Big Stump into pieces and move it.

Around 1918, the Petrified Forest and Cripple Creek Touring Company offered tourists the chance to ride Stanley Steamers from Colorado Springs to the gold-mining town of Cripple Creek, stopping at the petrified forest along the way. In addition to the Big Stump, the attraction's staff uncovered at least three new large petrified stumps. By 1922, Coplen owned the Hill property outright. He had the station of the old Colorado Midland Railway, now abandoned, moved by horses from the town of Florissant to the site of the Big Stump, a distance of about two miles. It was later remodeled and expanded into a lodge, with a large fireplace constructed out of pieces of petrified wood. Coplen records that his establishment had about three thousand visitors in 1924, but by then he was eighty years old and finding it difficult to spend time at such a high elevation.[16] After forty years of involvement, he decided that it was time to start looking for a new owner.

The big white lodge was well furnished when the property was sold to Palmer J. Singer and his wife Agnes in 1927. The Singer family owned the land and operated the Bronco Dude Ranch, which doubled as an active cattle ranch, and the Colorado Petrified Forest for forty-six years. During the 1930s, they attracted tourists not only to see the fossils, but also to spend a few days on the ranch. Vacations there sometimes included rodeos, horse racing, and gambling on slot machines. The resort employed more than twenty people during the Great Depression, but closed during the American involvement in World War II, reopening in 1946. When the dude ranch became too much work, the Singers concentrated on the petrified forest, attracting up to twenty-five thousand visitors there annually during postwar summers. Eventually the Singers noticed that visitors were walking away with more and more petrified wood, and the family decided to confine public fossil collecting to a wide trench dug into the shale beds near the lodge.

Just over a quarter of a mile away from the Singers, David and Ira Henderson developed the property they had purchased in 1920 into another petrified forest concession. They started digging in 1921 or 1922 where some petrified wood projected above the ground. It was hard work, but with the help of a horse and blade and a few sticks of dynamite to get through the hard volcanic rock, they excavated the unusual "Redwood Trio" and several huge stumps nearby. One of these, at 13.5 feet (4.1 meters) in diameter, was even broader than the Big Stump and still ranks among the largest-diameter petrified trees in the world, though it is badly fractured, perhaps by the dynamite used in excavation.

The Hendersons constructed a museum in 1924, and their large, drive-through covered gateway couldn't be missed by tourists driving along the county road. For many years, the Florissant Fossil Beds National Monument, continuing its long wait for new facilities to be constructed, used the historic museum as a visitor center.

When John Baker bought the Henderson property in the early 1950s, a bitter feud developed between him and the Singers. Each used aggressive promotions and trick signs to try to attract the most visitors. Singer is said to have stood in the road and tried to divert visitors into his driveway first. Concerned that tourists would drive into Singer's place first, Baker decided to plow a diagonal road across his property to create a new entrance right next to Singer's.[17] Singer responded by moving his own entrance farther north. The rivalry intensified, and local stories have it that when Baker went out one day to spread nails along the roadway to keep visitors out of Singer's place, he was wounded by a shot fired by one of Singer's guides.[18]

Another interesting twist in tourism's effect on Florissant's history has been reported by Toby Wells, whose family owned property along the eastern margin of the fossil beds.[19] Toby had grown up in Florissant, and as a boy during the 1950s, he worked as a tourist guide leading visitors around the Baker property, then known as Pike Petrified Forest. During the evening of July 11, 1956, a big car drove into the parking lot. A distinguished-looking gentleman got out and asked if he could take the tour. Toby explained that it was too dark to see much and that they were about to close, but agreed to take the man on a quick walk anyway. The lady in the car decided to remain behind. During the walk, the man asked if he could buy a large piece of petrified wood. Toby said that there were small pieces available for purchase in the gift shop, but the man pointed at a large stump next to the Redwood Trio and asked if he could buy it. Young Toby was stunned when the man introduced himself as Walt Disney. His wife, Lillian, still waiting in the car, began honking the horn and called out, "Come on, Walt, let's go, it's getting dark!" Disney met the owners and signed the guest register, and they agreed on a price of $1,650. The stump was later removed with a crane and shipped to California. Yet another of the ancient giants disappeared from the site.

Walt gave the stump to Lillian as a thirty-first anniversary gift, and she later donated it to Disneyland. Today, that tree is an attraction in Frontierland at Disneyland Park, where it has been viewed by millions.

During the years of private ownership, the neighbors around the petrified forests struggled to grow crops in the high, cold mountain environment. The summers were warm enough to grow potatoes, oats, alfalfa, and lettuce. Terraces still visible today were cut into some of the rolling hillsides to help create more arable land. Some of these properties also contained part of the fossil beds and were designated in 1969 for inclusion in the new monument. The Pike Petrified Forest that Baker had run closed its gate in 1961 and the old museum was abandoned. The Colorado Petrified Forest of the Singers continued to operate through 1972, and soon thereafter was sold to the government, as mandated by Congress in the creation of Florissant Fossil Beds National Monument. Another commercial fossil-collecting site outside the monument's boundaries, known as the Florissant Fossil Quarry, is still run today by the Clare family.

Conservation: The First Stirrings

The extent of souvenir hunting raised concern early on about how the fossil beds might be preserved. In 1891, soon after the Colorado Midland Railway arrived, *The Mineralogists' Monthly* argued that "the expenditure of a few thousand dollars by the town of Florissant in securing title to the land, digging out the stumps and grading the ground, would make it a great point of attraction for curiosity and pleasure seekers."[20] Two decades later, the *Denver Post* reported that a movement was under way, inspired by the work of William Strieby of Colorado College, to have the area designated by the government as a state or national park.[21] About the same time, a professor visiting from London, John Farnsworth, called it "the greatest fossil field in the world" and called on the citizens of Colorado to recognize its priceless quality.[22] And in 1915, the year the U.S. government established Dinosaur National Monument in northwestern Colorado and northeastern Utah, the *Denver*

Times called for the similar preservation of Florissant to protect it from ongoing exploitation for private gain.[23]

The National Park Service acknowledged the potential worthiness of Florissant as early as 1920, but it took twelve years before the Park Service examiner actually visited the site—and the news wasn't good. In 1932, Roger Toll, the superintendent of Yellowstone National Park, submitted an adverse report, which was followed five years later by another inconclusive investigation.

Conservation hopes were raised again briefly in 1952 when a later superintendent of Yellowstone, Edmund Rogers, visited at the request of the secretary of the Interior to study the feasibility of adding Florissant to the national park system. The resulting 1953 report acknowledged the national significance of the lake shale deposits but concluded there was no imminent danger to the scientific value of the site.[24] The report claimed that the interests of the local landowners, particularly those of the petrified forest concessions, would be sufficient to provide adequate protection from vandals, as well as continuing accessibility for scientists and students. One of the main concession holders, the Singers, however, knew firsthand of the ongoing problem posed by theft of petrified wood from their land, and they longed for the government to purchase and protect it. Agnes Singer wrote to the Park Service in 1958 and to Secretary of the Interior Stewart Udall in 1961, offering her own property "at a reasonable price" while urging the government to act to protect the site in perpetuity.[25]

Over the decades, it was de facto preservation by private owners such as the Colorado Museum Association, John Coplen, the Singers, the Hendersons, and the Bakers that kept "The Forest," as the site was sometimes known, from disappearing altogether. Although limited fossil collecting had been allowed, a considerable portion of the original petrified forest and shale beds still remained intact when the efforts for enduring conservation of the area finally came to a head in the 1960s.

The National Park Service made careful studies of the site from 1959 to 1962 as part of a long-range effort to identify areas of significance that might be added to the network of national parks. These studies concluded that the fossil beds were nationally significant and threatened by the rapid encroachment of summer homes and other development.[26] They recommended that a 5,500-acre national monument be established as soon as possible and that it should include a large-scale paleontology research and excavation program that would provide scientifically sound and up-to-date interpretation for visitors. In 1962 and 1963, all thirteen of the fossil beds' landowners were contacted, and they responded with nearly unanimous general approval to the idea of preserving a large area of the valley. Local county commissioners were also supportive, but some powerful real estate interests had a quite different end in mind for the land of Florissant.

Chapter Two

Geologic Book Burning or Preservation?

〜

ESTELLA B. LEOPOLD

When the mountains are overthrown and the seas uplifted, the
universe at Florissant flings itself against a gnat and preserves it.
—*Arthur C. Peale, Hayden Expedition geologist, 1873*

UNIQUE FOSSIL BEDS OF EVIDENT BEAUTY AND INTERNATIONAL RECOG-
nition of their scientific importance, occurring in a remarkable landscape,
might seem a perfect place for the nation early on to establish a park or
national monument. But that did not happen, though there were calls for
Florissant's protection by scientists and even some local ranchers as early as
the late 1800s.

Instead, the valley became an economic temptation. The uniqueness of
the area was a pheromone for buzzing developers. Until the early 1960s, this
part of Colorado had been predominantly pastoral, dotted with small farms
and cattle ranches. However, storm clouds of development had begun to
appear on the horizon.

When the National Park Service first announced interest in the area in
1962, real estate developers eyeing the area accelerated their interest in buying the land and selling plots at a pretty price for summer cottages.[1] And
ranchers, especially those on the periphery of the proposed monument, saw

an opportunity to cash in. There was cause and effect: land values had been low, but after 1962 land values took an upward turn. If this continued, it would preclude moves to make the region a monument. If the fossil area were developed for housing, the potential national monument might become impossible.

Sprawling housing developments and profits to be made in real estate were consuming land across the country. But this was not just any land. The Florissant fossil area is unique, its value incalculable as a national resource. Allowing real estate development there, one scientist said, "is comparable to what we might think of as a geological book burning, especially devastating because there is only one irreplaceable volume on this subject in the universe."[2]

In my position at the U.S. Geological Survey (USGS), I could see what was already happening to ranch land in the area: real estate values were indeed going up and subdivisions were appearing. Beatrice (Bettie) Willard of Boulder's Thorne Ecological Institute was noticing the same thing. Beginning in 1964, we began to work with environmental organizations and the press to try to stay the real estate development and ownership fragmentation of the Florissant valley (figure 2.1). Our springboard for action was the introduction in 1964 of the first bills in Congress proposing the creation of a Florissant national monument.

If enough people would join an effort to save Florissant, we thought, perhaps the public could exert enough pressure to bring Congress to act on the bills. But in an economy of rising land values, would it be in time? Most of the land within the boundaries of the proposed monument was still owned by ranch families, so there was a chance that the main part could be saved from development if Congress would act with relative speed. Bettie worked on the issue through the local Sierra Club chapter in Boulder, and I through the Colorado Mountain Club in Denver.

Florissant: A Personal Story of Science and Action

For me, the idea of conservation activism came from my father, Aldo Leopold, an early ecologist who was one of the first proponents for saving wilderness areas. He was a strong advocate for conservation all his life. His book, *A Sand County Almanac*, spelled out an ethical view of land and became a foundation text for American environmentalism.[3]

When my siblings and I were young, Dad bought 80 acres along the Wisconsin River, where we as a family spent many happy years repairing

Figure 2.1. Colorado Mountain Estates is a real estate development of A-frame cabins in the south end of the Florissant valley. This development was built during the mid-1960s. (Photograph by Estella B. Leopold.)

damage (now called "ecological restoration") on the worn-out land of our farm. We lived for those weekends close to nature spent camping at the rustic family cabin. As a youngster I spent many an idyllic day roaming the floodplain, chopping wood, learning plant names, swimming in the Wisconsin River, and playing on its beaches. The Sand County farm was a wonderful place to "get lost" in nature—a place to learn natural history.

I got to know Bettie Willard in the 1950s when I was studying for a master's degree in botany at the University of California at Berkeley. Bettie was teaching school then and living at the International House on the Berkeley campus. Later, she worked on her doctorate in botany at the University of Colorado, studying alpine plants at Rocky Mountain National Park, and became an active conservationist. She loved nature and would wax poetic reminiscing about her youth in the scenic California foothills of the Sierra Nevada where she grew up.

As a botany doctoral student working with conservationist Paul Sears at Yale, I learned to extract pollen and spores from recent muds in postglacial lakes in Connecticut to determine recent vegetation history there. With degree in hand, I arrived in 1956 at my new job at the USGS in Denver. In becoming acquainted with ecologists in Boulder, I was pleased to meet up again with Bettie, who was then working on her doctoral dissertation on alpine plants (figure 2.2).

I first came to learn about Florissant through my scientific work at the USGS. I was told that government geologists needed help in estimating the age of rocks in the Rocky Mountain area. It was my daunting assignment to try to develop a way to use fossil pollen and spores from ancient sediments for that purpose. As plants evolve in geologic time, their pollen features tend to change only slightly, making them useful to identify what plant groups they represent. Studying assemblages of pollen grains in mixes representing different plant associations was a new way to study fossil floras, and identifying the flora would help in determining the age of the rocks.[4] By studying pollen from a wide range of rocks in the region, some of which were of known age, I could put together a time sequence of pollen types for the Rocky Mountain area.

Figure 2.2. Bettie Willard at her Cut Rock research site in the tundra of Rocky Mountain National Park in 1961. She was marking tiny alpine plants with toothpicks and keeping track of their success over time. (Courtesy of National Park Service, Rocky Mountain National Park, Dr. Beatrice Willard Collection, ROMO-1689.)

First, I needed to extract pollen from rock and, second, determine stratigraphic sequences of floras for rocks of known Cenozoic age (the last 65 million years). The idea was to mimic microfossil techniques that German scientists used for determining stratigraphic sequences in mining coal, and that oil geologists also used on their drilling cores to tell one layer from another. However, none of these scientists seemed to know how to—or bothered to—identify the plants represented by the pollen in their samples. As a botanist, I wanted to use—and did build—a modern pollen reference collection as an aid for botanically identifying the pollen in fossil floras to decipher what the ancient forests were like. I eventually found that the pollen suites of the early Cenozoic era (post-dinosaur interval) were easy to discern from pollen in the younger middle Cenozoic rocks. Further, many pollen from the younger suites could be identified down to the genus and also had a character of their own.

To get started, a colleague at the USGS office in Denver handed me a piece of rock from the Florissant valley—I remember it had a nice plant leaf preserved on it—and asked if I could extract pollen from it. It did not take long to discover that not only could I extract pollen from the Florissant sediment, but also that it was beautiful stuff. Furthermore, I found I could identify many of the fossil pollen types by comparing them with pollen of living forest genera.

In my first report for USGS, I expressed my wonderment that, in a single small piece of rock, I found beautiful and abundant pollen grains, thousands of them, and these pollen grains were evidence for a multitude of familiar plant genera. The data yielded an enticing picture of the vegetation and flora that existed at Florissant some 34 million years ago! It was exhilarating. There were conifers such as spruce, pine, fir, and sequoia types, and many familiar hardwoods such as elm, hickory, maple, oak, ironwood, and hackberry (figure 2.3). There were aquatic plants such as cattail; herbs such as evening primrose, grasses, and ferns; and shrubs such as greasewood and soapberry. With further collections from different geologic sites, some of which were of known age, our efforts in the laboratory soon began to provide evidence revealing evolutionary sequences for the development of early Rocky Mountain forests in the Cenozoic. We were matching rock age with pollen floras.

The next step was to go to Florissant and make further collections to increase our understanding of the flora there and to trace changes in the site's vegetation through time. We collected the first suite of sediment samples from the big road cut near the town center. Then we sampled other areas, such as the fossil "fish beds" just east of the petrified forest area (figure 2.4).

While I was preparing a paper on the Florissant flora at the Ecological Society of America Meetings in the 1960s, I met Harry D. MacGinitie, the famous paleobotanist of the University of California at Berkeley who had written a monograph on the Florissant leaf flora in 1953.[5] Working on Florissant pollen and spores got me started on a career of sampling microfossils from a wide range of sediments in the American West in order to construct a history of floral evolution and plant changes in the region.

When the absolute radiometric age of the Florissant beds, 34 million years, became known in the 1970s, we used the Florissant pollen flora as a benchmark for that period in the geologic history of the southern Rockies. I sampled for pollen at other western sites where the geologic age was

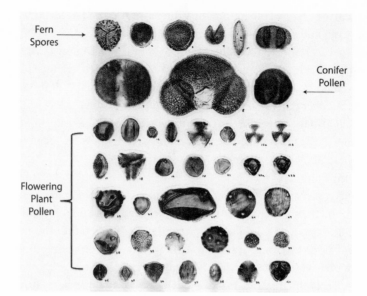

Fern Spores

Conifer Pollen

Flowering Plant Pollen

Figure 2.3. Photographs of fossil pollen grains prepared by Estella Leopold from an outcrop of Florissant lake sediments. The pollen micro-fossils are tiny, ranging from 20 to 150 microns in size. These are actual cell walls of pollen that were preserved in fine volcanic ash that fell into Lake Florissant in the late Eocene. Many of these can be identified to modern plant genera. (Photograph by Estella B. Leopold.)

established through fossil mammals or isotopic dating. At my lab we began to assemble a kind of chronology of pollen floras through the Cenozoic era. USGS geologists started sending me rocks whose ages were unknown, and for these we could estimate age using fossil pollen from previously dated sites. In the eyes of the USGS, the method was successful and helpful, so the agency eventually hired two other pollen specialists in the ensuing years.

Changes on the Land

While engaged in scientific work, I couldn't help but notice changes that were occurring in the Florissant area. Real estate developers in the early 1960s were quick to buy up and begin development on some 2,400 acres along the periphery of the proposed monument. By 1967 it was pretty clear that the Park Service was likely to buy up the Florissant valley eventually.

Figure 2.4. A group of paleobotanists from the U.S. Geological Survey collecting fossils at the "fish beds" locality near Twin Rock Road on July 15, 1960. Left to right: Richard A. Scott, Genie Doher, Alan Graham, and Estella Leopold. (Reprinted with permission from Alan Graham.)

By that time, certain ranchers had become deeply concerned about the future of the area, as described in chapter 1. They wanted to see the fossil beds preserved, not subdivided. Prominent among these ranchers was a matriarch of the valley, Agnes Singer, and her family (figure 2.5), owners of the Colorado Petrified Forest, which represented about one-half of the local area of petrified trees.

"It was my husband's dream to have it become part of the National Park system, and come under the protection of the [Park] Rangers," Agnes told Estelle Brown of the Rocky Mountain Sierra Club chapter in a 1969 interview.[6] I visited their 800-acre ranch and got to know Agnes's son, Bob Singer, who ran the operation in the 1960s. Like his mother, Bob was dead set on seeing the area become a national monument. The whole family cared deeply about the fossils and the importance of stopping vandals from dragging the fossil wood away. A deep pride was evident in Agnes's voice when she spoke of the fossils, of the Singer family's commitment to preservation, and responsibility for a trust.

"In earlier days," Singer remarked, "people came just to see, to wonder. Now there is much more interest in

Figure 2.5. Agnes and Palmer J. Singer were the owners of the Colorado Petrified Forest from 1927 to the early 1970s. This photograph was taken around 1951. (Photograph courtesy of Tim Singer.)

fossil history, in studying the science, in facts and in finding their own." But vandalism had increased, too, a prime reason she hoped the state or federal government would come in to protect the region: "The rocks were simply disappearing. At one time there were big petrified stumps and logs lying on the ground all around the countryside around Florissant. But they have mostly been sold or stolen away. Broken up for souvenirs. . . . [T]ourists began sneaking in under the fence and taking all they could carry."[7]

Motions in the House

In 1964, at the urging of citizens like Agnes Singer of Teller County (the county in which the fossil beds are located), Colorado congressman J. Edgar Chenoweth drafted the first bill to designate a national monument in the Florissant area. The Colorado Springs Chamber of Commerce supported the proposed monument as a tourist attraction, and Teller County officials promoted the plan. Geologists from the Smithsonian Institution and the Department of the Interior in Washington, D.C., also backed the idea of preserving the fossil beds.

Chenoweth introduced House Resolution (H.R.) 11834 on June 30, 1964, in the Eighty-Eighth Congress. The bill proposed a size consistent with that of a 1962 NPS report, 5,500 acres, but it died before any action was taken. A year later, Chenoweth's successor, Frank Evans, introduced a similar bill, H.R. 8032, to the Eighty-Ninth Congress. Creation of a national monument would entail passage of a bill by Congress that directed the NPS to purchase appropriate land and establish an office at the site. Ultimately, the NPS would establish an interpretive center where the public could learn about the paleontology of the Florissant beds.

Once Congress was showing interest in these bills, a path was set. Clearly, most of the national monuments established for the NPS were created by presidential proclamation; for example, Teddy Roosevelt created ten national monuments between 1906 and 1908. An exception in recent times was the establishment by an act of Congress of the Mount St. Helens National Monument for the Forest Service in 1982. As this Florissant story unfolds, readers can see the stark difference between the two types of origins for our national monuments: congressional action versus presidential proclamation.

Protecting fossil-rich areas was not a new concept for the NPS. Dinosaur fossils, for example, were discovered in northwestern Colorado in 1909, and

Figure 2.6. Colorado Mountain Club members collecting fossils at Florissant, 1965. Note the thin slabs of shale called "paper shales," which were layers of sediment in old Lake Florissant. (Photograph by Estella B. Leopold.)

the Dinosaur National Monument was established there in 1915, with its huge vertebrate fossils. The area has been protected ever since.

At the Colorado Mountain Club, I chaired the Conservation Committee, which met regularly and encouraged club members to write in support of the Florissant bill. We also led many field trips to Florissant to acquaint club members with the wonderful resource that Florissant represents, the nature of the fossils there, and the local geology (figure 2.6). I sent a letter on behalf of the Colorado Mountain Club to Representative Wayne Aspinall in 1966; we invited him—in fact, we urged him—to visit Florissant so that we could show him the area. I reported to him on the work the club members had done to interview local ranchers, and I described our interest in the future monument.[8]

Support for these early legislative proposals was spurred by geologist Eleanor Gamer, who was teaching at Colorado College. After leading her own field trips, she wrote an enthusiastic article in a 1965 issue of *National Parks* magazine that touted Florissant as a potential monument: "It has been estimated that of 150 localities containing fossil insects, only the Baltic amber has yielded a greater number of specimens than have the little lake beds of Florissant. It would make a perfect companion area to Petrified Forest National Park of Arizona."[9] Support for the monument among the local ranchers had been rising ever since 1952 when Edmund Rogers's negative report to Interior had stimulated some of the locals to circulate petitions and write their members of Congress.

The Conservationists Rally

In 1964, Congress passed the Wilderness Act, which created a national system of protected wild lands. In Colorado, as elsewhere, we conservationists
were ecstatic and felt our testimony on behalf of the bill might even have
made a difference. It was a taste of success.

Buoyed by this enthusiasm, Hugh Kingery, who had been instrumental
in encouraging local wilderness bill efforts at the Colorado Mountain Club,
began recruiting members, including me, to work on other current environmental issues. In Colorado at the time, environmental folks of all stripes—
young and old, skiers, hikers, mountain climbers, businesspeople, geologists,
ecologists, botanists—were beginning to recognize the effects of a wide
range of new, politically charged natural resource conflicts that were developing in the West and the importance of working together to address them.

In Colorado it was Ed Hilliard, the managing partner of the Redfield
Gun Sight Company of Denver, a Wilderness Society board member, and a
devoted conservationist and mountain climber, who initiated the effort. On
September 27, 1964, about one hundred Colorado conservationists gathered
at the first Open Space Conference to discuss collaboration. Ed called on
Roger Hansen, a Denver environmental lawyer and land use planner, to help
us get started. Roger prepared a talk about the need for the nonprofit clubs
of Colorado to unite under an umbrella organization. He spoke about a blueprint, a plan of action for our efforts to help with statewide planning and
land-use control. He proposed that we form an umbrella group to enable us
to work together more effectively.[10]

All the major outdoor groups came to this historic meeting—the garden
clubs, bird clubs, Wilderness Society, Mile-Hi Alpine Club, Colorado
Whitewater Association, Trout Unlimited, Colorado Mountain Club—you
name it. During the conference, Ed pulled about ten people from the audience, including Roger Hansen and me, and conducted a few sessions asking
us to discuss how we could build an umbrella group to coordinate work on
environmental issues. The Colorado Open Space Coordinating Council
(COSCC) was the name we all chose. It was the progenitor of today's Colorado
Environmental Coalition.

The steering committee (Ed Hilliard, Estelle Brown of the Sierra Club,
and myself for the Colorado Mountain Club) met at Ed's office many times
with Roger Hansen, who was hired to serve as staff and draft a constitution
and bylaws. Ultimately, representatives from twelve groups assembled. With

much tugging, pulling, and arm-twisting, seven groups decided to officially join together as the COSCC on April 6, 1965. Member groups included the Colorado Mountain Club, the local chapter of the Sierra Club, the Garden Clubs of America chapter, and the Wilderness Society. Soon COSCC had a statewide following, and similar umbrella organizations took root in a number of other states.

Among its first actions, COSCC (later COSC) took a position favoring the passage of Representative Frank Evans's Florissant bill. Members of the Sierra Club chapter and the Colorado Mountain Club, after field visits that we led to Florissant, became enthusiastic supporters of the Florissant bills. Evans's initial bill, however, sat in committee and was never reported out to the House floor. On June 16, 1966, Evans wrote to Roger Hansen: "We have been waiting for some time for the Park Service to file its report with the House Interior and Insular Affairs Committee but as of this date have not been successful in this regard. . . . [T]he Committee cannot do anything until it has received this report and the time remaining in this session is running out." [11] On June 20, a *Denver Post* editorial headline read "Florissant Project Still Petrified."

Despite this setback, public momentum for the monument grew during the spring and summer of 1966. On June 15, with the backing of its now-numerous member groups, COSCC issued a press release supporting a new Evans bill and extolling the great value of the fossil beds.[12] Evans replied with a message of appreciation. My Colorado Mountain Club Florissant-oriented Conservation Committee met to plan our approach to the print media, television, and radio, and to recruit letters of support from the public. We now had club members actively helping on the Florissant issue in the major cities between Boulder and Pueblo, and friends in sister organizations in Colorado Springs organized publicity in the Pikes Peak region. We were continuing to lead field trips to the area.

To build greater public interest, several of us—Bettie Willard of the Thorne Ecological Institute, Estelle Brown of the Sierra Club, geologist Roger Morrison of the USGS in Golden, Colorado, and I—each led repeated field trips to Florissant (plate 2). We brought the press along, too. During the spring of 1966, we took ninety-six conservationists into the field to see the fossil beds. One member of the Colorado Mountain Club, Susan Marsh, came on our spring field trip. As it happened, she wrote for the *New York Times* and produced a good story about the Florissant fossil beds that came out that July.[13] We were excited to see publicity for Florissant (and our pictures) in the Sunday edition. Her story noted: "The fossils at Florissant show the evolution and modernization of insects perhaps better than any other known site in America. The remarkable abundance of the fossils, and the perfection with which even the smallest details are preserved, makes these fields especially significant." In December another person from our earlier field trips, Henry Lansford, published a feature story in the *Denver Post*'s Sunday edition entitled "Treasure in Stone," sparking additional public interest.[14]

Rising public concern about Florissant generated a great deal of further coverage in the media, which was fortunate for us and brought new volunteers to our cause. We had significant coverage and editorial support from the Denver and Colorado Springs papers, which gave us regular full-page and photographic coverage. These were effective because, after all, Florissant fossils are very photogenic! Over four years' time, the articles in the press and the flow of letters to Washington, D.C., helped to focus congressional attention on the need for protection of the fossil beds.

As support for the Florissant monument grew in 1966, so did threats to the fossil beds. During that summer, I wrote an article for the Colorado Mountain Club's *Trail & Timberline* newsletter anxiously alerting our members about the encroaching real estate developments.[15] I was among many who wrote Colorado representative Wayne Aspinall to express our concern that a second real estate development, Crystal Peak Estates, had begun building in the north margin of the proposed national monument. The effect of these developments was to skyrocket land values in the whole area, including the portion that the government might have to buy for the monument. Even worse, we were told by one of the local ranchers that the eastern half of the proposed monument was soon going to be put up for sale to the highest bidder. The situation was becoming very serious.

The National Park Service Gets Busy

The initial event that prompted the National Park Service to move on Florissant protection was action taken by the Advisory Board on National Parks in 1962. The board gave their support to the draft proposal for making the fossil beds a national monument, based on the 1962 NPS pilot report and plan.

Still, it wasn't until September 1964 that Granville Liles, superintendent of Rocky Mountain National Park, and Larry Knowles, NPS park planner, had visited the area with the regional chief of proposed park studies and others.[16] They met with the Teller County commissioners to test the waters and visited local landowners in the Florissant valley. I was asked, as a member of the USGS, to join them and discuss what my assistant, Carol Lind, and I had found to determine the presence of fossil deposits within the proposed southeastern boundary.

The early (1962) outlines of the proposed 5,500-acre monument included the whole central part of the Florissant basin and a large segment of a ranch owned by Nate Snare on the south end of the basin. Yet this proposed acreage was only about a third of the total area of the Florissant Formation. On a weekend in 1964, Carol and I paced out the southeastern margin of the basin looking for fossils and entered on a topographic map the places where we could find Florissant lake beds and fossil wood. It was apparent that the lake beds extended about four miles farther south than was recognized by the 1962 report, and some arms of the fossil formation reached in different directions as much as a mile or two beyond the locations shown in the report—far more than seemed possible to include within the proposed monument boundary. We felt that the monument should certainly include the major collecting localities of historical importance in the valley. To help Larry Knowles, we turned over to him the map Harry D. MacGinitie had published that showed the total extent of the Florissant lake beds (see figure 0.1).[17] The planners found that a number of landowners, but not all, were willing to sell at an adequate price. One of the boundary issues that came up at that time concerned the land of Nate Snare (figure 2.7), who was the great-nephew of early settler David P. Long. Snare's land, which lay just two miles south of the main petrified forest area, included some nice fossil beds and fossil woods. I had visited a number of times, collecting fossils there with his permission. Nate was a fine person and I respected him.

Figure 2.7. Rancher Nate Snare and his wife at their farmhouse holding a slab of Florissant *shale* displaying a fertile branch of *Sequoia affinis* that has small, male, pollen-bearing cones on it. (Photograph by Estella B. Leopold.)

Snare pleaded with the Park Service not to include his land in the proposed monument, at least for the time being. "I can sell to these subdivisions for one hell of a lot of money," he said, "but I don't want to. When I first bought this place in 1930 it was overrun with prairie dogs. The creeks had washed away the grass. I've made this place. I've filled in washouts and done things you can't see. After I've put in forty-some years here, I don't feel like selling."[18] There was only one way of life for him, he said, working his land, and that was that. Maybe when he got older, Nate conceded, he would not mind his land going into the proposed monument, but not now. The NPS agreed to leave most of Snare's land out of the proposal.

There was more to this story in later years, and it did not turn out well. In the 1980s, Snare said he was finally ready to turn over his land to the NPS. MacGinitie, the NPS, and I were preparing to visit him to clinch the deal when we learned the sad news that Nate had been killed in a car accident on the highway near Florissant. The transfer of Snare's land to the NPS never occurred, and the property remains outside the national monument.

In the fall of 1965, the Advisory Board on National Parks, Historic Sites, Buildings and Monuments had given the NPS another push, in the form of a short memo to the secretary of the Interior:

> In light of the time that has passed since the Advisory Board recommended [in 1962] the Florissant Fossil Beds for National Monument recognition and the outstanding value of the area, the Board expresses the hope that every appropriate action will be taken to achieve the purpose of the recommendation.[19]

In addition to the advisory board memo, senior scientists at the American Museum of Natural History wrote Representative Evans asking for action on the House bill. These were encouraging developments for us conservationists. But Congress could not act without a final master plan from the NPS outlining the monument's proposed boundaries and appraising the value of the land needed so that a budget could be established. That plan was still not completed.

In 1966, Ted Swem of the NPS (who told me he was an acquaintance of my father's) recruited a team from its San Francisco office, including Merrick Smith and Harry Robinson, to assess the terrain and estimate land values. The team in turn asked for my help because I knew the area and some of the ranchers. Thus it was that on a cold fall day with a biting wind, Harry Robinson and I found ourselves standing on the gravel road outside a pasture while Merrick Smith walked around inside the pasture dressed in a bright red wool shirt. Suddenly a large bull came out of nowhere and chased after him. Smith headed toward us as fast as he could with the bull right behind him. He made a dive under the barbed wire fence and managed to escape, but he tore his red shirt badly. I can remember Harry and I trying not to laugh, while I fished out another garment from my car to help protect him from the cold wind.

The following spring, on May 5, 1967, and with all documents finally in, the NPS issued a thirty-seven-page final master plan for the 6,000-acre monument, along with a map proposing the exact boundaries.[20] The plan clearly described the significance and the nature of the fossil beds. The NPS published a flyer summarizing the plan, which the COSCC immediately put to use to draw public interest in the monument idea.

Frustration in the House

In February 1967, Frank Evans introduced a new bill, H.R. 5605, to the new Congress that again proposed creation of the national monument, this time for 6,000 acres. He said he "had received hundreds of expressions of support from both organizations and the public-at-large. I have yet to see signs of opposition at all." Evans mentioned COSCC's strong support and pointed to our statement claiming that the Florissant beds were "one of the world's outstanding natural museums of historical plant and animal life."[21]

Three months later, H.R. 5605 unexpectedly came up for a House Ways and Means Committee hearing, the first hearing of any kind on the monument proposal. We conservationists learned of the hearing only sixteen hours in advance, not enough time to send a representative to Washington, D.C., to testify. This meant that the Florissant bill was in front of the committee without its champions, making the bill especially vulnerable to alteration. And altered it was. Arkansas representative Wilbur Mills, chairman of the House Ways and Means Committee, in a move toward economy, said he could see "no good evidence" that the monument needed to be so large. He and James A. McClure of Idaho emasculated the bill by cutting the monument size to only 1,000 acres and slashing the funding to only one-third of the original amount. In this greatly diminished form, the bill tiptoed through the House and to the Senate where it sat.

In shocked response, the COSCC submitted an extensive statement to a
large number of congressional members explaining the importance of securing a 6,000-acre monument, not just the 1,000-acre version. A monument so
small would include only the immediate area around Singer's Colorado
Petrified Forest and Baker's Pike Petrified Forest, yet it would leave the surrounding fossil beds open to housing development (figure 2.8).

On September 5, 1967, the assistant secretary of the Interior wrote
Representative Wayne Aspinall to weigh in on the same side:

> We have serious reservations as to the adequacy of an area such as
> would be provided in the bill as amended by the Committee. The
> revised boundary now encompasses only one arm of the former
> lakebed, protects very few of the outcroppings or historic digs
> where the fossils are exposed at the surface, and accords only mini-
> mal protection against adverse developments which could encroach
> upon the monument scene and destroy irreplaceable resources.[22]

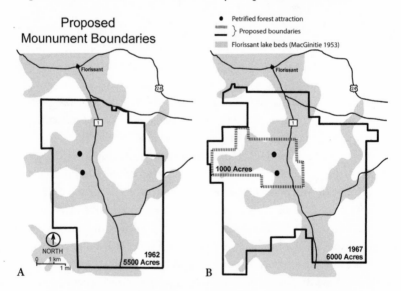

Figure 2.8. Two maps showing the proposed outlines of the Florissant monument.
The National Park Service pilot study of 1962, which proposed 5,500 acres (A). The
National Park Service master plan of 1967, which proposed 6,000 acres (B). In 1967,
the House of Representatives passed a bill for a diminished monument of only 1,000
acres (area enclosed in dashed line in B). This would have included only the land
close to the petrified forest area (black dots). (Map drafted by Lindsay Walker; courtesy of Florissant Fossil Beds National Monument.)

Other conservationists, of course, were exercised as well. Bettie and I each wrote personal letters to the congressional delegation in fierce opposition to any bill proposing less than 6,000 acres for the fossil beds, as did many others. After the emasculated bill passed the House, I received a letter from Representative McClure claiming that the committee had been given little information about the proposed monument at the time of passage. How could that be, I wondered, given the growing mound of documents from citizens, organizations, and the NPS in support of the larger monument?

Senatorial Stirrings

In March 1968, COSCC issued a full-blown description of why 1,000 acres would be completely insufficient to protect the main fossil areas and the important outcrops.[23] It discussed the development costs, and the escalating prices of land in the valley. The message was that the federal government should authorize purchase of the land now, before it was too late, and postpone the expense of developing monument facilities until later if necessary. This was followed by a full-blown explanation from the Natural Areas Committee of the University of Colorado about a document that we helped draft at the USGS office asking "Why should the proposed monument be 6,000 acres in size? Why not 1,000 acres?"[24]

To date, Colorado's senators had not shown much interest in the Florissant issue. Bettie had been corresponding with both senators, Gordon Allott and Peter Dominick, urging them to visit Florissant and to draft a bill for the Senate. It was the COSCC press releases and Bettie's letters to the Colorado delegation, I am convinced, that prompted the senators to take some action. I found a letter from Stanley Cain, assistant secretary of the Interior for Fish, Wildlife and Parks, indicating that Senator Allott had asked him to answer some questions about Florissant.

Allott had apparently asked about plans for reducing the monument to 3,000, 2,500, or even 1,000 acres. As Cain saw it, Allott wanted to avoid having a monument designation that might "upset the local economy any more than necessary."[25]

In the same letter, Cain commented to the NPS director:

It seems to me that Florissant offers the Service an opportunity for original, imaginative and possible unique policy that would provide for the usual visitor services and in addition allow further excavations for scientific purposes, including both research and student training, and, under proper control, provide for public rock hounding also. . . . Why not consider starting with simple facilities, with expansion as visitation warrants?[26]

Cain also wrote to Allott, answering many of his lingering questions and seemingly allaying some of his fears. How fortunate we were that Stanley Cain, an admirable person and an internationally known plant ecologist, was serving as assistant secretary of the Interior at that time.

Allott, then chair of the Republican Party, proposed to visit the area in person on May 10, 1968. We were thrilled! Roger Hansen, Bettie Willard, and I drove down to Florissant early that morning. The senator's helicopter appeared through a cloud and landed at the petrified forest area. After exchanging greetings, we eagerly drove him to the best fossil plant localities and showed him the petrified stumps, including the Redwood Trio at Baker's place and the Big Stump at the Singer ranch. We also showed him the proposed boundaries of a 6,000-acre monument outlining the scenic basin. He seemed to be energized by all he saw and expressed enthusiasm about his trip. Only ten days later, Allott entered Florissant bill S. 3524 for consideration by the Senate and the Ninetieth Congress. That was fast work!

Commenting on the bill, its co-author and Allott's fellow Colorado senator, Peter Dominick, said we should take into account the government's tight budget situation: "I would urge that we first and foremost preserve the total proposed site; purchase the 6,000 acres and develop the museum, service buildings, and roads at a later date. We must act now, affirmatively and effectively, or the opportunity may well be lost."[27] Allott had said much the same to us during his inspection of the area. His words sounded all right to us; good enough as long as the fossil beds were saved!

On February 3, 1969, Colorado representative Donald Brotzman, supported by Frank Evans, reintroduced a 6,000-acre monument bill, H.R. 5953, into the Ninety-First Congress. Two days after that, Bettie sent Brotzman a copy of the statement by the University of Colorado Natural Areas Committee, with a strong endorsement from the faculty, and again explained the scientific importance of the Florissant area.[28]

In early March, Bettie also wrote to Wayne Aspinall asking him to permit the Evans/Brotzman bill out of committee to the House floor for a vote. That plea fell on deaf ears. On March 10, Aspinall wrote back:

To be perfectly honest with you . . . I personally felt that a good case was not made for the entire 6000-acre tract. I was depending upon the Senate to pass the bill and then take it to conference. This, however, failed to occur.

This year the committee is inclined to let the Senate act first. It is my personal thinking that if the Senate acts first and puts in the 6000 acres, then my committee may look at the value of the additional acreage in a more friendly light.[29]

In early February, our two Colorado senators entered a modified Florissant bill, the eventful S. 912. In his presentation to the Senate, Allott said:

My personal hope is that the ultimate preservation of this area will be accompanied by imaginative planning appropriate to the uniqueness of this area. I can well visualize that this approach would lead to the possibility of creating a living museum out of the Florissant fossil beds dramatizing new ways of displaying these fossils without necessarily incurring prohibitive expense for the construction of buildings and roads.[30]

He claimed that his visit to the area reinforced his conviction that the setting aside of 6,000 acres was absolutely essential to protect the best and most important parts of the area. The bill found a good deal of support.

About this time, Agnes Singer commented to Estelle Brown:

We keep hoping for Congressional approval of the Monument this year, because time seems to be running out for hopes of preservation. When the Park Service first proposed a 6000 acre parcel the local landowners were all agreed on selling to the Federal government. But the developers and speculators have moved in on us since then; many of the ranchers cannot or will not wait; the stakes are too high and the fossil lands are going to speculation, summer homes and immediate profits. Which seems too bad a fate for 40 million year old [sic] insects and leaves and trees![31]

As Singer spoke, she pointed to the east of Snare's ranch where, just out of sight, a burgeoning development of small wooden A-frame cottages stood, many of them summer homes (see figure 2.1). The process of land development in the area was well under way.

Singer's observation about the fate of the fossils certainly was true in spades. Sprouting "subdivision" and "for sale" signs worried us greatly as we went back and forth to Florissant. Driving westward toward Florissant that year, we passed a piercing orange billboard announcing WESTWOOD LAKE ESTATES. A little farther along was a sign for TROUT HAVEN ESTATES 2-1/2 MILES. South of the proposed monument was COLORADO MOUNTAIN ESTATES. 1/2 ACRE LOTS. Then, WAGON TONGUE HOME SITES—FLORISSANT. Near Florissant, south of U.S. Highway 24, were the signs reading, LOTS $15 DOWN. $15/MONTH and 4 SEASONS FUN WILDERNESS ESTATES. Ever since the NPS publicized the idea of a national monument at Florissant, land prices had been getting hotter and more speculative.

Ted Thompson, superintendent of Rocky Mountain National Park, stated in a *New Yorker* magazine article: "This country is changing fast. That's why we're fighting so hard for the Monument. We think it's now or never. It used to be just tourists here. They'd stop and then drive on. Now it's subdivisions— vacation houses. Everybody wants an A-frame in the mountains."[32]

Meanwhile, Bettie in Boulder and I in Denver were giving public lectures to increase interest in the Florissant issues. In my talks to the Rocky Mountain Association of Geologists and to the Denver Audubon Society at the Denver Museum of Natural History, audiences expressed real enthusiasm for the full-scale monument proposal and many asked how they could help. Florissant was such a wonderful, exciting theme. It was especially easy to tell the story at conferences with good photographs of fossils in support (figure 2.9). This was a real "whodunit" mystery. There were the bad guys, the good guys, the reluctant Congress, and the scary loss of a spectacular public resource to real estate moguls. How was it going to turn out? We wished we knew.

Figure 2.9. Estella Leopold distributing information about the Florissant fossil beds story on the campus of the University of Wisconsin before a lecture she gave there. (Photograph by Milton Leidner; reprinted with permission of the Wisconsin Academy of Sciences, Arts & Letters.)

In March 1969, we had drafted a position statement explaining the need for support of S. 912 and again requested Aspinall to permit the Florissant issue to come before the House for a vote. Roger Hansen edited this statement for the COSCC board to consider.[33] It got full support from the member citizens' groups, and so Roger sent it off to the press and to Colorado's congressional representatives. We did this because we knew that a large piece of land within the proposed monument was up for sale to the highest bidder.

Then, on the evening of May 23, 1969, a bomb dropped. Bob Singer (Agnes Singer's son) called to tell us that the Gregg tract, comprising the eastern 1,800 acres of the proposed monument, had been put under contract to sell to a newly formed real estate firm, the Park Land Company of Colorado Springs. We had better act fast before the sale was closed, Singer advised. I remember sitting by my Denver phone in the dark, scared and horrified, calling Bettie in Boulder to tell her the bad news.

Chapter Three

The Developers Want Florissant

❦

ESTELLA B. LEOPOLD

THE CENTRAL PART OF THE FLORISSANT VALLEY, RECENTLY PURCHASED by A. W. Gregg of Houston, Texas, comprised some 3,000 acres, of which 1,800 acres had been proposed for inclusion in the national monument (figure 3.1). Gregg had originally purchased the land from John Maytag some seven years earlier, about the time the National Park Service first issued a plan for the national monument. Gregg originally supported the monument proposal and had turned down earlier bids for sale to private owners because each year, for seven years, he anticipated action by Congress. Gregg was now very elderly and his health was deteriorating. On Friday, May 23, 1969, a neighbor of Gregg's at Florissant, Bob Singer, called Gregg and learned that he had a contract to sell this tract to the Park Land Company of Colorado Springs. The price was around $450,000. This news had gradually leaked out to local ranchers.

Apparently a number of real estate men from Central Enterprises Company of Colorado Springs had established the new Park Land Company. Ray Thornton, speaking for the land company on July 4, 1969, indicated that the resale price would be twice the amount paid in purchasing the land from Gregg. Thornton referred to "obligations," which made it necessary for the company to start resale immediately, "either to private investors or to a holding company for the National Park Service."[1] In response, various groups supporting the national monument proposal promptly accused the company

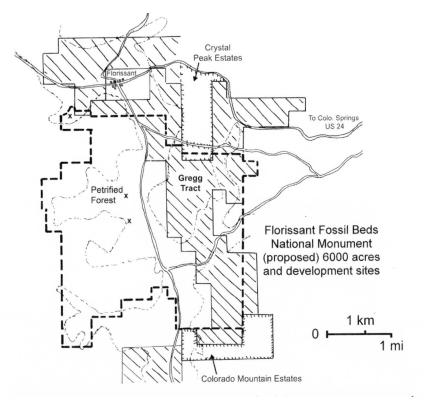

Figure 3.1. Map showing the proposed boundaries for the 6,000-acre monument and the Gregg tract (shaded area) that was under contract for sale to the Park Land Company in 1969 (after the National Park Service proposal, 1967 master plan). Note the outlines of two previous real estate developments (ca. 1965) along the margins of the proposed monument: Colorado Mountain Estates and Crystal Peak Estates. (Drafted by Estella B. Leopold and Stephanie Zaborac-Reed.)

of anticipating profit taking at the expense of the government. But the Central Enterprises Company claimed: "We have been negotiating for this property for almost two years and *were not aware the U.S. Park Service* was interested in a portion of this land until we had completed our purchase agreement" (emphasis added). In late May 1969, the *Colorado Springs Free Press* quoted Thornton as saying, "We're not being unreasonable on the price we're asking."[2] He said the company was asking a price that would cover only the original purchase and associated expenses. Even though proposals had been placed before Congress (1964) and were pending, Central Enterprises declared, "We cannot sit idly by for six months or more to see if

[the] legislature approves the request for the Florissant Fossil Beds. We must act."[3] Other than for economic speculation, the question of why the investors wanted to buy the land in the first place remains unanswered to this day.

Fossils Need Lawyers

In the spring of 1969, *Science* magazine and other media outlets published reports about a remarkable, exciting lawyer whose motto was "Sue The Bastards!"[4] The lawyer was Victor John Yannacone, jr., of Patchogue, New York. At thirty-one, he had just won a decision to ban the use of DDT in Wisconsin for ecological reasons.

"That's our kind of guy!" Bettie Willard and I decided. If we can find him, we thought, we'll ask him to help us get Florissant into the courts to challenge the Park Land Company against future subdivisions. I got busy tracking down a phone number for him. Early the next morning, I was excited to get Yannacone on the phone. I tried to explain the case to him. He asked some questions and said he would consult with his colleagues at the Environmental Defense Fund (EDF), a small group of activist lawyers and scientists who had supported Carol Yannacone's lawsuit to stop the indiscriminate use of DDT in Suffolk County, New York, to see if they would back him to work on the case. If he took the case, he would have to come to Colorado, he said. Could we pay his way? I said yes, wondering where Bettie and I would get the money.

Yannacone turned out to be the perfect choice. Luther Carter, writing in *Science* magazine, later described him as "a bustling, flamboyant lawyer with a brash style . . . an aggressive ringmaster and general counsel"; he has "a love of rhetoric and the center stage . . . a quick grasp of scientific information," which make him a terror to polluters and other wrongdoers.[5] Of him, EDF founder Charlie F. Wurster Jr. once declared, "Vic really thinks he can save the world. He's a brilliant guy."[6] According to those who had seen him in action, there was reason to believe he could!

Soon Yannacone called again. It was doubtful that EDF would sponsor the case, he said, but he would take it on individually. When should he come? "Right away," I said. "Get me a hotel room, then," he said.

On May 26, 1969, Victor arrived at the Denver airport. To my surprise, he had brought his wife Carol and their young son, Victor. We put them up at the ritzy Brown Palace Hotel in downtown Denver. The next morning, a fine spring day, I drove them to Florissant to look at the fossil beds. They happily dug for fossils in the northernmost part of the Florissant Formation (figure 3.2; plate 3) and were impressed with what they saw and learned at the site.

Figure 3.2. Victor Yannacone and his wife Carol digging fossils at Florissant on May 27, 1969. Notice the layered sediments representing the old lake bed. (Photograph by Estella B. Leopold.)

As we drove back to Denver, Yannacone instructed me about the possible case. "First," he said, "you and Bettie have to pull together about ten of the most prestigious scientists and civic leaders in the community to form a new group called Defenders of Florissant, Inc. Next, in order to prepare for court action, you and Bettie have to draft a brief for the court case." I asked what a "brief" was. "Okay, you write out a description of the recreational, scientific, historical, aesthetic, and evolutionary values represented by these fossil beds in nauseating detail! Got that? Third, you have to get me a local lawyer who can share the representation on this case with me. Someone you can trust and think highly of." He explained that an out-of-state lawyer needed to have representation from an in-state lawyer to file a court case in Colorado. Yannacone was impressive and enthusiastic, and we were delighted to have him on our side.

Defenders of Florissant, Inc.

That same day, Bettie and I got together to plan our efforts and began making our Colorado contacts. Time was pressing. We needed to put together a special activist group that was willing to legally defend the threats to Florissant. Who should we include as our local lawyer, and who should the Defenders be, and when could we all meet? We went over some names and immediately came up with Richard (Dick) Lamm, an environmentally notable and highly respected young lawyer serving in the Colorado legislature. We knew Lamm from his conservation work with the Colorado Mountain Club, including legislation to regulate billboards in Colorado. Here was the perfect person to work with Victor Yannacone. To our delight, Dick accepted the role. His brother and law partner, Tom Lamm, agreed to help with some of the details.

As the other Defenders of Florissant, Bettie and I chose Roger Hansen, executive director of the Colorado Open Space Coordinating Council (COSCC); Richard Bradley, professor of physics at Colorado College; the admirable state senator John Bermingham; John Chronic, professor of geology at the University of Colorado; Dick Beidleman, professor of biology at Colorado College; Bob Weiner, chair of the Grand Canyon Workshop; conservationist Ed Connors of COSCC; and a few others. Yannacone and Dick Lamm laid plans to file suit in the Federal District Court of Denver on July 3, if possible. Yannacone was optimistic that he could secure a "stay on the bulldozers" hired by the real estate developers if we had a sympathetic judge.

The Defenders had their first meeting on the afternoon of May 28. We met at my house to discuss how the group would work together. On Yannacone's instructions, we made lawyer Roger Hansen chair of the Defenders of Florissant, Inc., and Bettie was to serve as secretary. I was told to stay out of the Defenders because I was a Department of Interior employee. Yannacone wanted to be able to call on me for a deposition if necessary and later as a witness for testimony in court without creating a conflict of interest for me with the National Park Service, which is a branch of the Interior Department.

In case the legal approach failed, Bettie and I were also trying to find a source of major funding to perhaps buy the huge Gregg tract that fell within the boundaries of the proposed monument—1,800 acres under contract for $150 per acre to the Park Land Company, which informed the Defenders that they wanted more than twice that much. The Nature Conservancy had turned us down by saying that the required sum of around $540,000 was much too large. Bettie was in touch with Huey Johnson, a well-known conservationist in the San Francisco Bay area known for his ability to raise a great deal of money for environmental protection projects. I was also in touch with the El Pomar Foundation of Colorado Springs, one of the largest and oldest private foundations in the Rocky Mountain West, which was known for its grants for community stewardship and had assets totaling more than $550 million, but we were not getting any takers for the huge amount of money needed to buy the property.

Nervous that the National Park Service might not know what was happening on the ground in Colorado, Bettie and I had both written detailed letters to George Hartzog, director of the National Park Service, explaining the great danger to the Florissant valley and the proposed monument.[7] We told Hartzog that the papers for the sale of the eastern third of the monument would probably be completed on Tuesday, May 27. The developers had planned on delaying for ten days the building of roads in the area, during which time they would be open to selling the land to willing buyers (at twice the price that they paid for it). I did not receive any response to my letter, though I was able to discuss it with associate director Ed Hummel during the May 29 public hearing. At our urging, similar letters went that week to Director Hartzog from the Colorado Department of Natural Resources and the Board of County Commissioners of Teller County. Russ Train, undersecretary of Interior, also wrote Wayne Aspinall on May 26 to recommend, with small amendments, the passage of the current House bill on Florissant.

With the Defenders of Florissant born, we were all preparing for the Senate hearing scheduled for May 29 in Colorado Springs. This important event would be the opportunity for the senators to hear opinions from the general public about S. 912. On the drive back from Florissant on May 27, Yannacone had asked what I was going to say at the public hearing. I rattled on about the significance of Florissant fossils in understanding the evolutionary sequence of Rocky Mountain floras, the climatic implications, and other matters. He said, "No good, Estella. You have to do better than that!" So I tried again. He said, "No, you must broaden your message. Give it a try." I struggled again, still with the emphasis on science. And he said, "Now what are the *real* values of Florissant to the public and to posterity?" I shall never forget his grilling me, and of course, it was critical to try to appeal to the public conscience with our testimony.

After I delivered the Yannacones to their hotel that night, I stayed up to compose my message for the hearing. It was all about putting A-frame cabins on top of one of Earth's ancient treasures and about the fantastic field experience the Florissant valley offered. It was a challenge. I was sure Bettie Willard and Roger Hansen were struggling with their statements, too.

The Hearing

The Senate field hearing took place in the Little Theater of the Colorado Springs City Auditorium. We all dressed for the occasion and drove down to the city early. Senator Alan Bible of Nevada, chair of the Subcommittee on Parks and Recreation, presided, and Colorado Senator Gordon Allott and the staff representative for Senator Peter Dominick were present. The hearing was attended by a distinguished assemblage of congressional members, scientists, government officials, civic leaders, and important local citizens. The protagonists were loaded for bear, so to speak. Bible opened the proceedings by announcing that the morning would be devoted to testimony and that he was looking forward to an inspection trip of the fossil beds themselves in the afternoon. A national monument should, he said, using a National Park Service definition, "embrace a sufficiently comprehensive unit to permit public use or enjoyment of the scientific features or assemblage of features consistent with the preservation of said features." From the descriptions furnished by his colleagues, Bible said, "[the area] meets all the criteria with some to spare."[8]

The Senate bill under discussion, S. 912, would appropriate a sum of $3.2 million (later amended to $3.72 million) for the acquisition of a 6,000-acre national monument, and for necessary development and personnel for the first five years of the proposed program. This included funds for a paleontologist, a park naturalist, and a caretaker, among other things.

Senator Allott was the first to testify. He stated unequivocally that the monument should include 6,000 acres, not 1,000 acres. Then Senator Dominick's statement was read into the record, also asserting that the monument should not be smaller than 6,000 acres. Approval of S. 912 was an urgent matter, he said, and referred to a map showing the real estate developments that had already been popping up on the very borders of the proposed monument.

Following testimony from elected officials, a string of twenty-three well-known people spoke or submitted written statements strongly in favor of preserving the fossil beds as a national monument. The witnesses, one by one, built an overwhelmingly unanimous, diverse, and personally appealing plea for the monument. Conspicuously lacking were voices of dissent. Senator Bible asked a great many questions about the distance from Denver and from Colorado Springs, the number of cattle on the land, and the main land uses in the area. Speaking for the National Park Service, Ed Hummel provided many of the details. Thirteen landowners were involved, he said, and ten farm residences, though only two of the farms were used year round. As many as twenty-six thousand visitors were recorded at the Singer ranch each year.

A representative of Colorado governor John A. Love spoke, followed by state senator John Bermingham of Denver. Bermingham recalled his mother's description of a huge petrified slab of fossil wood that was used as their dining room table, which his family was convinced came from Florissant. Realizing that the state could do little to protect Florissant through purchase because of minimal resources, Bermingham had introduced a bill into the 1967 Colorado state legislature, senate bill 385, which described the metes and bounds of the fossil beds area and at least declared it a site of great scientific interest. Any heavy equipment used in the area without a permit from the Colorado Game and Fish Department was declared a misdemeanor. Landowners within the area were to have their property tax rate reduced. Though the proposed bill seemed a great idea when it passed the state senate, it died in the house.

When it was his turn to testify, Teller County commissioner Joe Burns read a letter the Entomology Department of the American Museum of Natural History had sent: "Florissant is a magic word known to scientists throughout the world for one of America's treasures. . . . In this small area are preserved in readily available form more species of terrestrial fossils than are known from anywhere else in the world."[9]

The turn of Harry D. MacGinitie, the famed paleobotanist from the University of California at Berkeley, came soon thereafter. MacGinitie, who had written the definitive monograph on Florissant plants and was still considered the leading authority on Florissant at the time, also stressed Florissant's international reputation. "[T]he fossil beds are widely known over the world for the wealth of fossil plants, insects, and fishes which they contain," he said. "The combination of life forms, their abundance and their beautiful preservation is unique. . . . The contrast between the environment of the present and that shown by the fossils, the climate and vegetation, is practically absolute."[10]

"This brings us to face a question of values," MacGinitie continued. "The land occupied by the lake beds is not of particularly great value, either for housing or agriculture, but as a page of earth history from the dim past it is priceless. You can't put a price on it, there isn't anything else like it. The area is unique and unrivaled. I know of no other spot in the world which has just the combination of all the ancient life remains that are found at Florissant and it is well known over the world. My colleagues in Europe and Japan, when they come to visit the United States, always want to know where the Florissant beds are, and want to visit the Florissant beds. There is hardly an elementary geologic text that does not mention the Florissant fossil area."

Mac showed the senators his book on the Florissant flora, published by the Carnegie Institution in 1953. "You mean we can have this book, Doctor?" Bible asked. The scientist responded, "No, you can't have it." (I knew it was his only copy!) Bible then said, "You mean I can look at it, but I have to give it back to you?" "Eventually, yes," said Mac. The two went on to discuss the fossil palm leaf and its importance, as well as the unusual abundance of *Sequoia* stumps.[11]

The next person to present testimony was Bettie, introduced as Dr. Beatrice E. Willard, co-chair of Thorne Ecological Institute. She told those assembled about visiting the Italian town of Pompeii, once buried in volcanic ash, and why it was a good analogue between more recent times and the much older valley of Florissant. The Florissant beds, she went on, were "comparable in the record of life on this planet to the Dead Sea Scrolls of biblical fame, the Rosetta Stone that unlocked the secrets of the ancient Egyptian civilization, the Gutenberg Bible that records the first Western printing." With urgency in her plea for prompt action, she concluded, "Can we even contemplate [any action except] prompt, immediate approval and attendant action to create here a jewel in the National Park Service—[thus] preserving intact one of the world's absolutely priceless scientific treasures? . . . Will we be too little and too late? We certainly face this imminent possibility."[12] As the morning passed, I grew more and more impressed by the dedication of those who came from near and far to testify. The hearing embodied a prime example of American democracy at work.

Then, it was my turn. My pitch was on the educational and aesthetic value of Florissant for the public:

> The story of evolution . . . is a pretty stirring and acceptable concept. [If you] tell a tale of post-Eocene evolution . . . on the flanks of the old Lake Florissant with the fossil quarry spread out before you, the eyes of the people from seven to seventy are sparkling. [You see that] the old Oligocene [sic] landscape is still at hand, with minor

changes, as a stage and the fossils are the actors. [But if you] tell the same story in the lab; show the same kinds of fossils to the same kinds of people and they think you are talking about science, and the drama of Florissant history doesn't come through. [If you] eliminate the stage and put the fossils under glass with typed labels—it is like drawing the curtains on the drama.[13]

I talked about having led many, many people to the field at Florissant to show them the spectacular setting of this 34 million-year-old lake, describing how the lake formed and pointing out the tremendous array of fossils there—literally a whole ecosystem of them—and what they can tell us of the history of life. I spoke as a botanist, as a student of fossil floras in the Rocky Mountain region: "Florissant fossils are perhaps most noteworthy because they span the interval from 34 to 38 million years," thereby bridging "an otherwise huge gap in the plant record of the region" that is singular in our history—the last subtropical warm period before our climate cooled suddenly at the end of Florissant time. And, in response to a question of Senator Allott's, I suggested that with some careful excavation at the site, visitors could walk up hill, level by level, and see a series of steps in evolutionary time. I concluded with this statement:

Today when the new society is tossing out remnants of past cultural patterns, it may seem unpopular to bother with saving a priceless scientific field library like the Florissant paper shales with all of their fine print. But I ask you, how can man keep a perspective on his direction and life's path if he loses track of the routes that life has followed before him? How can man evaluate his planetary environment and visualize his historic place in it if he does not keep and cherish a few touchstones with the past? When we have studied the moon, will we throw it away?

What you do about the proposed Florissant National Monument, gentlemen, will be a matter of history. . . . It is a historical observation that founders of Yellowstone Park and Grand Canyon National Monument, for example, are long remembered for their foresight, while those that opposed, no one ever hears about anymore.

If Florissant is not given national monument status this year, I fear all we will have is its old address.

The scientists who spoke that day all described how they used the study of the fossil beds for their classes or for environmental field trips. In a different vein, when Ruth Weiner, representing the COSCC, stood up to testify, she rattled off the names of twenty-three member clubs or groups that whole-heartedly supported S. 912. The senators were duly impressed.

In his remarks toward the end of the morning session, Richard Beidleman of Colorado College clearly summarized the Florissant situation on the ground for the senators:

> The Florissant beds represent a page of the world's geologic history book opened to a unique chapter of the Oligocene [sic] setting in America. From this chapter, for example, has come the most complete picture of fossil insects in the New World. Destruction of such a site is comparable to what we might think of as a geological book burning.
>
> There are a number of national monuments and national parks in the United States which preserve fossil remains. But no such preservation exists within the State of Colorado; and throughout the national park system, which attempts to display the many pages of our country's geological history, pages dealing with this particular portion of past life on earth are lacking—and may never be displayed if no action is taken at this time.[14]

Other academics giving testimony included Peter Robinson, professor of geology at the University of Colorado who stated that, despite large existing collections, "[d]etailed scientific excavations using modern statistical methods and controlled excavating techniques have not been made [at Florissant, and m]ore useful information . . . will be derived from future work. [This] would be impossible if the deposit were destroyed by development."[15] John Chronic, also a professor of geology, told us: "I have taken hundreds of University of Colorado students . . . to this unique area. . . . My thoughts turned as early as 1956 to efforts to get [it] set aside as a monument."[16]

Finally, Richard Bradley, a physicist at Colorado College and a member of the National Parks Association, made the following classic statement:

[W]e have here a most unusual circumstance, perhaps without precedent in recent legislative history; namely, a proposal is being made to put a substantial piece of land under the protection of the National Park Services [*sic*], and it stands virtually unopposed. Contrast this with the long bitter battles that raged over the creation of a Redwoods National Park or a Marble Canyon National Monument. If this bill fails to pass, it will not be because powerful lobbies were arrayed against it, but because this Congress, deeply involved . . . at home and abroad . . . could not seem to find time to consider it. . . . We hope you gentlemen will not allow it to happen. . . . [T]he preservation of prehistoric fossil beds may be deemed an insignificant issue compared to those other desperate problems. But it is not insignificant, as the sponsors of this bill well know; for the greatness of America lies not just in its genius to get men to the moon and back, but rather in the sum total of all the experiences and opportunities it can offer its people. The freedom—or the opportunity—to decipher the story of the earth from the messages encoded in rocks is as important to our culture as the freedom to use a public library.[17]

Senator Bible said he understood the urgency of the situation. He commented at the end of the morning's hearing that he felt "a little lonely" that there had been no opposition to the monument in the hearing. The only slightly negative tone came in a letter Agnes Singer and her son Bob, as owners and operators of the Colorado Petrified Forest, submitted for the hearing record establishing that they were not in agreement with the government's low valuation of their properties.

At noon the senators hosted a luncheon for a small group of public officials, as well as Harry MacGinitie, Bettie, and me, in the Ramparts Room on the fifth floor of the Antlers Hotel in downtown Colorado Springs.

After the luncheon, the senators and several officials drove to Florissant for the field trip, which was our chance to show them the beauty of Florissant. Even though we all were in our Sunday best, MacGinitie, Bettie, and I managed to show the officials around, dig a few fossils, pull out hand lenses, and talk about the importance of the beautiful fossils they were digging. It was quite festive. The press came out in force to photograph the event (figures 3.3,

3.4, 3.5). It was exciting to walk among the fossil stumps with the senators. And it was marvelous to have the famous "Mac" MacGinitie of Berkeley there with us (figure 3.6).

The next day the *Rocky Mountain News* ran a story about the hearing entitled "Will It Be Fossil Beds or More A-Frames?" It was illustrated with field photos and described the parade of witnesses pleading for the establishment of the 6,000-acre national monument. Ten days later, *Science* magazine came out with a short but powerful and supportive editorial by Philip M. Boffey entitled "Famous Fossil Beds Are Endangered" that described beautifully the stressful situation at Florissant to a national audience.[18]

Figure 3.3. After the public hearing of May 29, 1969, senators Gordon Allott and Alan Bible and staff went on a field trip to dig fossils at Florissant. (Reproduced with permission from the *Denver Post*.)

Two days after the hearing, we at COSCC announced a Florissant financial crisis and an accelerated fund-raising campaign. Some proceeds were required to pay the lawyers, their travel, and certain court costs, and much more might be needed to purchase the Gregg tract, priced by the realtors at the extraordinary sum (for those days) of $540,000. For the lawyers alone, we had to raise a minimum of $2,500 to cover expenses for Dick Lamm and $3,500 for Victor Yannacone.

Intermezzo

A relative quiet settled over the Florissant campaign after the hearing. We now had time to put more pressure on the House of Representatives and pursue funding. We got out another flyer on June 12 urging our audiences to "write your Congressmen and Senators" supporting the bills dealing with Florissant. I put together a long list of paleobotanists and paleontologists from Harvard to Berkeley and sent our publicity around. Even during this quiet period, the media continued to be a tremendous help in arousing public sentiment. Out of California on June 15, for example, came an article on

Figure 3.4. Senator Alan Bible with Estella Leopold (left) and Bettie Willard (right) discussing a fossil, May 29, 1969. (Reproduced with permission from the *Denver Post*.)

Florissant and the importance of monument status by Elizabeth Rogers in the *Sierra Club Bulletin*. It reached a lot of people nationally. On the same day, an editorial entitled "Preserve the Florissant Fossil Beds" appeared in the *Rocky Mountain News*.

To our delight, on June 20 Bettie and I each received great news by telegram; mine read as follows:

JUNE 20 69 5:23 PM EDT.

DR ESTELLA LEOPOLD, COLORADO MOUNTAIN CLUB

DELIGHTED TO REPORT S. 912, AUTHORIZING THE ESTABLISHMENT OF A 6000 ACRE FLORISSANT FOSSIL BEDS NATIONAL MONUMENT PASSED THE SENATE TODAY. I APPRECIATE ALL THE WORK YOU PUT INTO THIS MATTER AND KNOW THAT YOUR TREMENDOUS ASSISTANCE DURING FIELD HEARING CONTRIBUTED TO SUCCESSFUL PASSAGE OF THIS BILL. THANKS AGAIN, AND BEST REGARDS

GORDON ALLOTT UNITED STATES SENATOR

The *Denver Post* headline read "Florissant Fossil Beds Bill Cleared." The bill authorizing the national monument had passed in the Senate with flying colors. "This bill was pushed through faster than any I can remember since coming to Washington," Senator Allott told the *Denver Post*.[19] It had been

Figure 3.5. The Big Stump with Bettie Willard and colleague (left) and Estella Leopold and visitor (right), 1969. (Reproduced with permission from the *Denver Post*.)

only four months and two weeks from introduction to passage. Senator Clifford Hansen of Wyoming opposed the 6,000-acre monument and the new bill, but he was talked into not voting, which was the closest thing to dissent in the whole affair. Other than this abstention, the vote was unanimous. The vote was exciting, of course, despite the five years of stalled efforts in Congress to get it. Now we needed a vote in the House.

On the previous day, the Teller County commissioners took a stand in support of protecting the area of the proposed monument. They passed a resolution that the lands in Township 13 S, Range 70 W and 71 W (the location of the Gregg tract), "shall not be subject to subdivision regulations" previously adopted and hence could not be subdivided.[20] Technically this local political action showed important support for the creation of a national monument in the valley.

For Want of an Abstract

It was sometime in June that the "abstract of title"—a document summarizing the details about ownership of a piece of land, including all conveyances and any burdens or charges on it—for the Gregg property somehow could not be found at the Teller County courthouse. A buyer usually wants to have this at the time of closing as assurance that there are no liens against the land that might sour the deal.

If the document had once been there, it had mysteriously disappeared. The Park Land Company needed the abstract to close the sale, and without a deed, the company could not begin development. The rush to development had stalled, at least for the moment. The Defenders were probably thinking "The Lord does his work in mysterious ways."

The moment did not last long. On July 2, in the midst of an annual Thorne Ecological Institute conference that Yannacone and several of us were attending in Aspen (figure 3.7), we learned by a telephone call from Tom Lamm that the Park Land Company was planning to close their contract with a "quitclaim deed"—in effect, a way to transfer a land parcel without a warranty of title. Not a minute could be wasted. We immediately packed and drove back to Denver to be ready for a court challenge to any impending changes on the land. Bettie had to stay behind because she was leading the Aspen environmental conference.

Dick Lamm filed a suit on July 4 in the Federal District Court on behalf of Defenders of Florissant, Inc., and the COSCC. The suit asked for a temporary injunction to restrain landowners from defacing the land set aside for the proposed monument. The *Rocky Mountain News* promptly ran a story with the headline "Group Seeks Injunction to Preserve Fossil Beds."

To clear the way for me as a federal employee to testify in court on the

Figure 3.6. Harry D. MacGinitie showing Senator Alan Bible how to collect fossils. MacGinitie was the author of the definitive scientific work on the Florissant flora and testified during the Senate hearing on May 29, 1969. (Reproduced with permission from the *Denver Post*.)

Florissant case, Dick Lamm had written to the director of the U.S. Geological Survey requesting his permission, which was granted. Victor Yannacone heavily edited my affidavit for anticipated use in court.[21] On Tuesday, July 8, I signed it hurriedly, and somewhat reluctantly, as not all of the expressions were what I would have used. Yannacone talked me into letting them use the version I signed because it had been given to Roger Hansen, who was ready

Figure 3.7. Bettie Willard organized an environmental conference at Aspen, Colorado, in July 1969 and invited Victor Yannacone (right) to speak. In this photo he is discussing environmental strategy with colleagues. The person on the left with dark glasses is lawyer Roger Hansen. (Photograph by Estella B. Leopold.)

to fly to Washington to bring our suit to the Supreme Court should their intersession be needed. Supreme Court justice Byron White of Colorado was an acquaintance of ours. We hoped to obtain his interest in the matter. This was a fallback plan, in case we lost the court case in Denver and were unable to appeal to the Tenth Circuit Court of Appeals. Our first hearing was scheduled for the next day, July 9, in Denver.

The night before the court hearing, I developed a major case of jitters and worry. Oh, how we needed to win!

Chapter Four

Fossils Go to Court

❧

ESTELLA B. LEOPOLD

Public sentiment is everything. With public sentiment
nothing can fail; without it nothing can succeed.
—*Abraham Lincoln*

ON THE MORNING OF WEDNESDAY, JULY 9, 1969, VICTOR YANNACONE,
Dick Lamm (figure 4.1), Tom Lamm, several other Defenders of Florissant,
and I, along with several friends from the Audubon Society, approached the
Federal District Courthouse in downtown Denver. The courthouse is an
imposing, Greek-columned, white stone building, and we entered the courtroom of Judge G. Hatfield Chilson with some trepidation.

The defendants, the Park Land Company, planned to excavate roads and
culvert ditches in preparation for real estate development on the Gregg tract
of the Florissant valley (see figure 3.1). Under the auspices of the Defenders
of Florissant, we were asking for a temporary restraining order and were in
court to show cause why such a restraining order should be imposed before
any development occurred. At the outset, Judge Chilson posed the question
of whether he even had the authority to issue such an order.

To address the fundamental issue of the court's authority, Yannacone
laid out the main arguments in the Defenders' complaint:

(a) The proposed Florissant monument is a national natural resource treasure,

(b) The sovereign people of the United States have the right to enjoy the unique values of the Florissant fossil beds without diminution and degradation,

(c) Degradation of this unique, national, natural resource treasure violates the rights of the people of the United States and unless restrained by the court, the Defendants will develop the area in such a way as to cause serious, permanent, and irreparable damage to the unique Florissant fossil beds. Road building, excavation, or covering the fossil beds with permanent dwelling units is not compatible with maintaining this national natural resource treasure, for the full benefit, use, and enjoyment of the people of the United States not only during this generation, but generations yet unborn.[1]

Yannacone pointed out that the defendants (the Park Land Company, Claude R. Blue, Kenneth C. Woford, J. R. Fontan, and M. L. Barnes) intended to commence construction immediately. He noted that the nature of the fossil beds was such that "the injury, which may be inflicted by the defendants if they are permitted to develop the area without regard for this natural national resource, will be irreparable in that it cannot be adequately compensated in damages."[2]

Yannacone's motion demanded that the court issue such orders as would protect the unique paleontological, paleobotanical, geologic, and palynological values represented by the Florissant fossil beds pending a final hearing and determination of the action. An affidavit I had prepared on the value of Florissant was included to support the complaint. Dick Lamm and Yannacone also submitted minutes from the Teller County commissioners' meeting

Figure 4.1. Dick Lamm was originally a member of the Colorado legislature and later became the governor of Colorado for three terms. (Reproduced with permission from Richard Lamm.)

of June 9 and their resolution stating that the Gregg property area should not be subject to subdivisions.

Making the Case

In stating the Defenders' case, Yannacone argued on constitutional grounds. Later, describing the Florissant litigation in his treatise *Environmental Rights and Remedies*, he wrote, "Legally, [the Defenders] argued that the right to preservation of the unique and irreplaceable Florissant fossils, [because those fossils were] a national, natural resource treasure, was one of the unenumerated rights retained by the People of the United States under the Ninth Amendment of the Constitution and protected by the due process and equal protection clauses of the Fifth Amendment, and the rights, privileges and immunities, due process and equal protection clauses of the Fourteenth Amendment."[3]

In addition, Yannacone asserted that "the Florissant fossil beds were subject to protection under the [Public] Trust Doctrine." He was referring to a principle of law with a very long tradition whereby the State, even the British Crown, had an obligation to protect certain resources for public benefit. As Yannacone put it, "[W]hile the defendants could profit from their nominal title to the land and make reasonable use of the area, they were under a duty to maintain that portion of the property vested with public interest, the 34 million-year-old fossil shales." He referenced the Fifth, Ninth, and Fourteenth Amendments to the Constitution, particularly the Ninth, which states that the rights *not* specifically enumerated by the Constitution are deemed to be retained by the people of the United States. He asserted that one of those unenumerated rights of the sovereign people of the United States is the right to the full benefit, use, and enjoyment of an irreplaceable natural resource. Because of its unique paleontological, historical, and scientific values, the Florissant area should be appropriately held in trust for the benefit of the American people.

Yannacone called on the federal court to exercise its traditional equity jurisdiction by invoking the centuries old maxim, "equity shall suffer no wrong without a remedy . . . unless restrained by order of this Court." Yannacone continued, "[T]he Defendants will develop the area to be included in the proposed Florissant Fossil Beds National Monument, in such a way as to cause serious, permanent and irreparable damage to the unique national natural resource treasure that is the Florissant Fossil Beds."[4]

Rendering a Judgment

Judge Chilson held that nothing in the U.S. Constitution prevented land-owners from using their property in any way not prohibited by law. He did admit that preserving the fossil beds was important. In addition, Judge Chilson refused to permit our attorneys to enter in the court record any supporting documents other than the papers submitted with the order to show cause that Bettie and I had helped prepare. We did not serve every single partner in the Park Land Company because some were traveling and unavailable. Chilson summarily dismissed our case. The ruling was a shock to us.

After Judge Chilson's decision that day, an informal conference was held in the hall outside the courtroom between Yannacone, Lamm, and me for the Defenders of Florissant, and the defendants' lawyer Robert Johnson and two of the Park Land Company partners, including Claude Blue. Judge Chilson had suggested the conference to see if the defendants would agree to some voluntary restraint of their bulldozers. Unfortunately, the road they planned to cut went very near the place I had shown to the senators as an ideal spot for a "walk through time" type of display similar to exhibits at Dinosaur National Monument in Colorado and Utah. The proposed road would destroy significant scenic values, we believed, as well as cut through the notable "fish beds" fossil locality (see figure 2.4).

The defendants, not surprisingly, said they doubted if the severity of the damage would be as great as I had suggested. Yannacone asked for time before the bulldozers would run, and they promised to delay the bulldozers only five days, until Monday, July 14. Once again they offered to sell the southern part of the potential monument land to our organization in the next three days for $350 an acre, but only if we could give assurance that very day that we would pay the price in full ($540,000). We, of course, did not have the money.

Just as the conference was breaking up, Yannacone announced we would appeal to a higher court (the Tenth Circuit Court of Appeals), and he held out a new motion. Johnson shot back, "Two of the four members of the Park Land Company are out of the country—just try and find us!" To which Yannacone replied, "Do you mean to imply that you don't think you have been served?" Yannacone was in effect officially notifying Johnson that we were appealing and that we expected him to appear. "Try and find us!" Johnson repeated. Yannacone raised his voice and extended the motion papers toward Johnson, saying, "Everybody be a witness! I am handing this Notice of Motion and Appeal of our case to Johnson." Johnson did not take it. Yannacone threw it on the chair next to Johnson and said, "Well, there it is. I'll see you in court." As we left, we heard Johnson and the two defendants snickering at us.

The Defenders of Florissant felt that the land company's "purchase or else" proposal was a form of community blackmail. Yannacone and the Lamms got busy preparing arguments for an appeal. For example, Chilson had not permitted us to enter a copy of the Florissant master plan into the court record. When Colorado State University graduate student James Thompson later wrote a paper on the Florissant case, he commented, "These development guys didn't know it, but they were trying to sandpaper a wolverine's nose."[5]

The next day the U.S. Court of Appeals for the Tenth Circuit heard our appeal. In conjunction with the appeal, Yannacone filed a motion to censure Judge Chilson for his courtroom behavior.

For the appeal to the Tenth Circuit Court, it looked at first like we were again in a bind. With two of the partners conveniently out of the country and a third nowhere to be found, it was impossible for the Defenders to give notice to all the partners of the Park Land Company in time. And serving one partner, the court had just ruled, was not adequate service upon the entire partnership, a technicality. Yannacone, however, thought such a strict construction of the rule could be challenged.

The Defenders' Appeal

On Thursday morning, July 10, Yannacone and the Lamms had drafted a reply to counterclaims raised by the Park Land Company. On his way to court to file the papers, Lamm received a telephone call (probably from lawyer Robert Johnson) full of bad language, cussing him out, but informally reporting that they would be willing to accept $350 per acre *not* to start bulldozing. They also reported that a bulldozer was poised, waiting for the court to resolve the issue, at the place on the Gregg tract where the developer's road would begin. Would the bulldozers roll into the fossil beds, win or lose?

The night before, Dick Lamm had driven to Colorado Springs with Mark Hogan, Colorado's lieutenant governor, to see Claude Blue. They found Blue leading a Democratic Party meeting. They tried to "talk some sense into him," as Dick put it, but to no avail it seemed.

On Thursday, July 10 at 2:00 p.m., the Defenders of Florissant and their attorneys, Yannacone and the Lamms, met again in the small, historic, wood-paneled courtroom of the Tenth Circuit Court of Appeals. Chief justice Alfred P. Murrah and associate justices Jean S. Breitenstein and John J. Hickey filed in, garbed in their long, black robes. The room fell silent in anticipation. With the Park Land Company partners and their lawyer nowhere in sight, Chief justice Murrah convened the court.

Yannacone presented a marvelous case for Florissant. He described the proposed road and the fact that the bulldozers might even swing into action that day or at least by Monday. He related our conversations with the Park Land Company and mentioned that they had offered us the chance to buy the land if we could produce the asking price of $350 an acre in cash within three days, even though the company had recently closed the deal with Mr. Gregg for $150 an acre with no cash down and no terms.

Judge Hickey questioned whether the Court had the authority to issue a restraining order in the absence of any statute protecting the fossils. Yannacone responded, "I must admit that Congress in its infinite wisdom has not seen fit to pass legislation protecting fossil beds in general. However, if someone had found the original Constitution of the United States buried on his land and then wanted to use it to mop a stain on the floor, is there any doubt they could be restrained?"[6] One of the judges then said, under these circumstances, he might issue a restraining order. Yannacone responded, "[W]hatever legal precedent you'd use there, I'm using here."

Yannacone told the court about the pending congressional action. The courts were the only way to stop the bulldozers and save the fossil beds from potential harm in the interim, he said. He presented a review of the scientific merits of the fossil beds and went through far-reaching arguments about how fossils, modern air pollution, and climatic change are connected.

With references to both the ancient and the divine, Yannacone closed with a flourish. He picked up a fossil palm leaf that had been uncovered on the Gregg tract at Florissant, and holding it up to the court, pleaded:

> The Florissant fossils are to geology, paleontology, paleobotany, palynology and evolution what the Rosetta Stone was to Egyptology. To sacrifice this 34-million-year-old record, a record you might say written by the mighty hand of God, for 30-year mortgages and the basements of the A-frame ghettoes of the seventies is like wrapping fish with the Dead Sea Scrolls.[7]

Then he sat down.

The judges asked a few questions during Yannacone's presentation, but we could not tell which way they were leaning. Judge Breitenstein suggested that the U.S. Attorney General could have been called on to stop the bulldozers, but Yannacone pointed out that there would be no authority for such an action until Congress had passed the bills creating a monument. The judges excused themselves for a "few minutes," which turned into a thirty-five-minute recess, as they apparently read our papers and held a conference. We stood outside the courtroom hoping and crossing our fingers. We were short of breath.

The judges reconvened the court. In a two-sentence ruling they said they had deliberated and decided to issue a temporary restraining order until July 29 when the case would be heard on its full merits in district court. They asked if Yannacone would draft an order that they could sign. I looked around the courtroom. The faces of the Defenders were wreathed in smiles, and there were many misty eyes. It was an electric moment. The court asked if we would withdraw the motion to censure Judge Chilson, and Yannacone declared he would be happy to do so. As we left the courtroom, Bettie and I hugged everyone. We all were very excited.

The restraining order issued by the three justices was unusual. The length of a stay was typically ten days or less, so at about eighteen days, this one was longer than customary. How lucky for us! It read:

> IT IS ORDERED that the defendants, jointly or severally, individually or collectively, or by their agents, servants or employees, their contract vendees or their successors in interest, be and are hereby restrained from disturbing the soil, subsoil or geologic formations at the Florissant Fossil Beds by any physical or mechanical means including, but not limited to excavation, grading, road-building activity or other construction practice until a hearing on the merits of the plaintiff's application for preliminary injunction to be heard in the United States District Court, District of Colorado, on July 29, 1969, at 9:30 A.M.

> IT IS FURTHER ORDERED that service of this order shall be made by the United States Marshal on any workman engaged in construction activities at the Florissant Fossil Beds forthwith and that personal service shall also be made on each of the defendants subject to the jurisdiction of the Court. Dated July 10, 1969.

Signed by: ALFRED P. MURRAH, CHIEF JUDGE, UNITED STATES
COURT OF APPEALS

JEAN S. BREITENSTEIN, JUDGE

JOHN J. HICKEY, JUDGE[8]

Yannacone had told the court that Florissant was an ideal case for judicial intervention because of the near unanimity of support for the monument among groups and government agencies. Included were the president (who was apparently ready to sign the bill), the Senate, the House of Representatives (to all appearances), the Department of Interior, the Budget Bureau, the local county, the state of Colorado, and the Defenders of Florissant, a large group of ranchers, and other enthusiastic supporters. Literally the only opposition to the plan was from the Park Land Company. Chief Justice Murrah's appeals court moved where and when no one else could or would.

The following day, the *Rocky Mountain News* published a story about the decision with a photo of Dick Lamm, Victor Yannacone, and me looking at a fossil. Under the headline "Court Order Halts Fossil Bed Project," they wrote, "In a precedent-setting ruling the three-judge court restrained Colorado Springs land developers from building an access road through the 34 million year old, world-famed area" (figure 4.2). They quoted Yannacone as saying, "This court can't countenance destruction of the 34 million year-old record, a record written (in stone)."[9] A Dan Gibson cartoon appeared in the *Rocky Mountain News* in June showing a series of stone markers carved with the names of several established national monuments, reminding us that many

Court Order Halts Fossil Bed Project

Figure 4.2. After the temporary restraining order was issued by the Tenth Circuit Court of Appeals, the story in the *Rocky Mountain News* was accompanied by this photograph of Estella Leopold (left), Dick Lamm (center), and Victor Yannacone (right) discussing the only palm leaf fossil found at Florissant. It is this fossil that Yannacone showed the justices in court. (Photograph by Mel Schieltz; reproduced with permission from the Denver Public Library, Western History Collection.)

Figure 4.3. "Tools for the Job" by Dan Gibson of the *Rocky Mountain News,* June 8, 1969. (Reproduced with permission from the Denver Public Library, Western History Collection.)

fine monuments had been created before this proposal. The stone marker for Florissant was incomplete (figure 4.3).[10]

The environmental lawyer Zygmunt Plater, in his 2004 book *Environmental Law and Policy: Nature, Law, and Society,* commented about this unique case: "The argument Victor Yannacone made for the restraining order was bold and innovative. It was also without precedent." Yannacone had made an eloquent case for why the people of the United States—as more than simply a term for the government—should have standing in a court of law. The judges did not make law by issuing a restraining order, but with their ruling they indicated that Yannacone's argument was worthy of serious consideration.[11] Concerning the unprecedented nature of Yannacone's argument, law professor William H. Rodgers Jr. claims, "Yannacone had no theory and he had no law. His only source of hope was his own rashness. His argument was a figment of his imagination."[12] Yet on Yannacone's creative argument hung the fate of the fossil beds. Yannacone insists today that "there was a theory—the Trust Doctrine of Equity Jurisprudence and the natural law basis for the Ninth Amendment—and there was law—hundreds of years of English common law equity all of which became a part of American Jurisprudence in 1796—or we would not have won. Precedents are necessary only when the law is well established."[13]

After the court proceeding, Roger Hansen (figure 4.4) called from Washington, D.C., and heard the good news. He was amazed. He had tried to reach Supreme Court Justice Byron White, but White's office did not seem anxious to act, or would wait for the lower courts to decide first.

Dick Lamm called the Park Land Company lawyer, Robert Johnson, that afternoon from the press room of the courthouse and was treated to a barrage of insults. Johnson angrily called Yannacone a New York Jew, a bastard, and other inappropriate names. He disparaged the importance of the case and verbally attacked Lamm, who, indignant at the way he was being treated, finally slammed down the phone in disgust and stormed out of the press room.[14] Despicable treatment is despicable treatment.

Later that day Dick Lamm called the relevant county officials we knew. He told them not to let the bulldozers move into the Gregg tract because the appeals court had issued a restraining order and the marshal would be serving the papers to the defendants within two days.

At 4:30 p.m. that afternoon, I put Victor Yannacone and his assistant on a plane to New York and went home to celebrate. The celebration, however, did not last long.

Figure 4.4. Lawyer Roger Hansen in the field. Roger was the co-designer of the Colorado Open Space Coordinating Council that became so politically active during the 1960s. (Reproduced with permission from Roger P. Hansen.)

Chapter Five

Victory—in Court and in Congress

§

ESTELLA B. LEOPOLD

THE TEMPORARY RESTRAINING ORDER OF JULY 10, 1969, FROM THE Tenth Circuit Court of Appeals was an unexpected blow to the private land developers intent on carving up the Florissant fossil beds. On the following Tuesday, July 15, Robert Johnson, attorney for the Park Land Company, and Claude Blue, a partner in the firm, filed a motion asking that the order of the appeals court be dissolved "on the grounds it violates substantial and fundamental constitutionally guaranteed property rights." According to the motion, "No precedent exists for authorizing the court to enter a temporary restraining order and enjoining land owners from making a lawful use of their land, merely because Congress may at some future time declare the area . . . a national monument."[1] The next day, the *Denver Post* ran the headline "Florissant Company Seeks to Kill Order."

At the time, no action seemed forthcoming from the House of Representatives to put the Florissant bill on the floor for discussion and potential passage. This lack of action could spell doom for the temporary restraining order, and ultimately for the Florissant site.

And then things began to move. On July 20, the *New York Times* published a persuasive story entitled "Fossil Beds in U.S. Go Unprotected—Government Fails to Act on Florissant Purchase." The story carried a vivid quote from Richard Beidleman of Colorado College: "Destruction of such a site is comparable to what we might think of as a geological book-burning, especially devastating because there is only one irreplaceable volume on this

Figure 5.1. Real estate sale signs along the Florissant valley increased in number over time, creating further worries about saving the fossil beds. (Photograph by Susan Flader.)

subject in the universe." *Science News* carried a story on June 21 entitled "A Treasure in Danger." Still at this time we were very aware that would-be monument land might still be sold to real estate developers (figure 5.1).

As the Defenders of Florissant, we were trying to raise money in earnest to pay for the mounting legal costs. We issued a one-page flyer featuring fossil insects and circulated copies to various groups under the title "Fossil Insects and Flowers Go to Court" (figure 5.2). The press aided our efforts by publishing announcements that our campaign was in "fiscal trouble" and looking for donations.[2] We set up an elaborate network of information and donation collection stations at several Colorado shopping centers. In Denver, these included five shopping malls, two grocery stores, and a department store. In Colorado Springs we had collection tables at five shopping centers, and in Boulder we had tables at three. Sandy Cooper of the Thorne Ecological Institute organized this effort, and the response was very helpful. To increase public awareness, we printed lots of green bumper stickers that said "Bail Out Florissant" decorated with a beautiful fossil dragonfly. It was fun to see these showing up around Denver and Boulder. The first environmental bumper stickers in Colorado were printed in 1963 to "Save Grand Canyon," so this was a second such use by our conservation groups.

The Wright Stuff

With only a temporary injunction in place, we were all anxiously preparing to go into district court again on July 29, when the full merits of the case would

FOSSIL INSECTS AND FLOWERS GO TO COURT

IN DEFENSE OF THE FLORISSANT FOSSIL BEDS

The "Trio" (Sequoia stump)

WHY?

A precedent setting decision on July 11th by the 10th Circuit Court temporarily restrained a group of Colorado Springs real estate developers from any type of construction on 34 million-year old fossils.

In a winning presentation of the unique educational and scientific values of the Florissant Lake deposits, N. Y. lawyer Vic Yannacone held up a fossil palm leaf before a three judge court and told them that to build A-grams on this singular natural, national resource would be like "wrapping fish in the Dead Sea Scrolls!" Representing the Defenders of Florissant, Yannacone and his co-lawyer, Dick Lamm, Denver attorney and legislator, won a remarkable restraining order to prevent bulldozing until July 29th. On that date the Federal Court will fully review the pubic vs. private claims.

The developers have filed a counter suit and promise that if the Defenders of Florissant lose the case, bulldozers will roll the next day.

A Congressional bill to form the proposed Florissant National Monument passed the Senate in June and is shortley going to the floor of the House. But will Congress act in time?

Figure 5.2. Fossil insects and flowers go to court (part of flyer). The Colorado Open Space Coordinating Council printed and mailed flyers to Colorado conservationists to keep them up to date on the progress being made to save the Florissant fossil beds. (Flyer redrafted by Jordan Holley; photograph by Estella B. Leopold.)

be heard. A few days before the court date, a Denver citizen, Vim Crane Wright (figure 5.3), called me. We had first met when I gave a talk about Florissant at the Denver Audubon Society a few months earlier. She had been following the case since in the press, she said, and wondered what we were going to do if we lost in court. I said, "Frankly, I don't know, but I am *hoping* we will win." If we lost, she asked, "What would you think if my lady friends and I went down to Florissant and sat in front of the bulldozers?" I said, "Great heavens, oh, you what? Well, we should certainly think about that." I said I would carry her intriguing idea back to several of the Defenders and see what they had to say.

I saw Bettie Willard and Roger Hansen that evening and asked them what they thought. Bettie looked amazed. Roger shook his head and said, "*Who* is this person exactly?" I said, "Well, I really don't know. She just wants

Figure 5.3. Vim Crane Wright in the field. Vim was an incredible leader who went out to "shake the trees" for the Florissant fund and managed to draw wide attention to our cause. (Photograph by Estella B. Leopold.)

to hold up the bulldozers, in case we lose." "Well," ventured Roger, "tell her maybe that's all right, but tell her just don't use our name [Defenders of Florissant]."

I reported back to Wright and offered to furnish her with a map showing the location on the Gregg tract where the bulldozers were supposedly parked and where some sympathetic ranch friends, the Snares, could be found in case she needed anything. Members of the Colorado Mineral Society, I learned, were planning to join forces and go with her to the site as well.

Vim Wright's team began their preparations. The team included Carolyn Johnson, then of the Denver Mineral Society; Mary Burton, a resident of the Denver area; pregnant Sally Story of Denver, with friend, Dona Ruth Buchan, and her young daughter, Holly Buchan; and others from Denver. They planned to meet in Colorado Springs on July 29, and Vim asked me to telephone them at a local radio station with news as to whether we won or lost in court that day. She also contacted representatives Frank Evans, Donald Brotzman, and Wayne Aspinall, telling them that she and her neighbors, including children, were going to block the bulldozers, and "they had better get that Florissant bill passed pretty quickly or she was going to be in real danger!"

Years later, Wright recounted in an oral history interview, "Then I thought of the enormity of what I volunteered for. I went right out and had my hair done, put on my pearls and high heels. I thought no self-respecting bulldozer driver would run over a woman in pearls and high heels."[3]

"Vim was the environmentalists' and the quality-of-life brigade's answer to a dream," Dick Lamm later commented. "She was a smart woman who had lots of time [for the campaign]. . . . The chorus—you always need a chorus. She was behind the scenes and organizing the people, making the drum beat in the press. I didn't do any of that. We just handled the legal part."[4]

A Legal Roller Coaster

On the morning of July 29, 1969, we Defenders all met at the Federal District Court and discovered we were back in the hearing room of Judge G. Hatfield Chilson. Yannacone again presented our case and asked the court for a preliminary injunction. Before the first witness was called, Judge Chilson called Yannacone to the bench and said, "I'm going to give you your day in court and then I'm going to throw you out on your fancy eastern law school ass. It's too bad you never learned anything about western law in that fancy eastern law school you went to."[5] The hearing then continued.

Plate 1. Contemporary view of the valley (Photograph by Lindsay Walker; courtesy of Florissant Fossil Beds National Monument.)

Plate 2. Colorado Mountain Club members collecting fossils (Photograph by Estella B. Leopold 1966.)

Plate 3. Victor Yannacone collecting fossils in 1969. (Photograph by Estella B. Leopold.)

Plate 4. Estella Leopold (left), Bettie Willard (center), and Vim Wright (right), the three women who were leading activists in the fight to save Florissant, posing near the petrified Redwood Trio during the twenty-fifth anniversary of the monument in 1994. (Photograph by Dorothy Bradley; courtesy of Florissant Fossil Beds National Monument, FLFO-272.)

Plate 5. The people central to guiding the Florissant case included (left to right) Estella Leopold, Tom Lamm, Richard Lamm, and Victor Yannacone, all of whom reunited at Florissant during the fortieth anniversary of the monument in August 2009. (Photograph by National Park Service staff; courtesy of Florissant Fossil Beds National Monument, FLFO-430.)

A

Plate 6. The two most famous petrified trees at Florissant are the Redwood Trio (A) and the Big Stump (B). (Photographs by Chuck Harvell [A] and Lindsay Walker [B], National Park Service staff; courtesy of Florissant Fossil Beds National Monument.)

B

A

B

Plate 7. Reconstructions of the streamside forest with large redwood trees and an understory of hardwood trees (A) and the volcanic mudflows coming off the slopes of the Guffey Volcano and flowing into the valley below, where they uprooted and buried large trees (B). One of these volcanic mudflows created a natural dam that blocked the stream drainage and caused the lake to form. (Artwork courtesy of the National Park Service, NPS/HFCCAC/Rob Wood.)

Plate 8. Reconstruction showing ancient Lake Florissant with the Guffey Volcano in the background. Cattails and roses grew near the water's edge, and a lush forest of conifers and hardwoods surrounded the lake. Woodlands and scrublands occupied the more distant drier hills. The rhinoceros-like brontothere (left) and primitive *Mesohippus* horse (right) were mammals known to inhabit the forest. (Artwork courtesy of the National Park Service, NPS/HFCCAC/Rob Wood.)

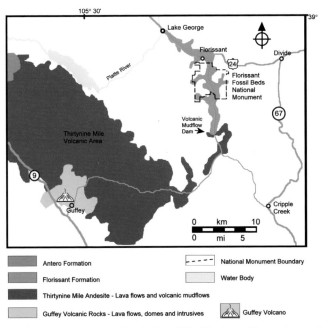

Plate 9. Geologic map showing the relation of the Florissant Formation to the rocks of the Guffey Volcano. Lava flows, domes, and intrusives were emplaced near the volcano itself, while volcanic mudflows and lava flows flowed off the broad flanks of the volcano to form the Thirtynine Mile Andesite. One of the volcanic mudflows formed a dam that caused the formation of Lake Florissant. Even today, the outline of the Florissant Formation reveals the general shape of this ancient lake. Another younger lake to the west became the site of deposition for the Antero Formation. (Map drafted by Stephanie Zaborac-Reed.)

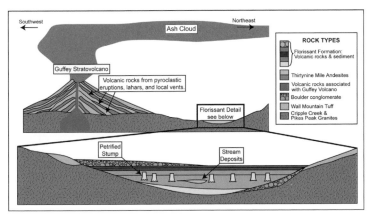

Plate 10. Cross section showing the relation of the Guffey Volcano to sedimentation in ancient Lake Florissant. A volcanic mudflow buried the bases of large redwood trees along a stream valley. Later, overlying rocks were formed in a lake and preserved the delicate remains of leaves and insects. (Illustration by Joseph Hall and Lindsay Walker; courtesy of Florissant Fossil Beds National Monument.)

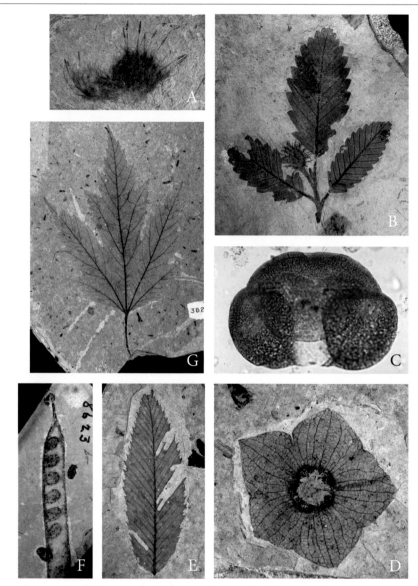

Plate 11. Fossil plants. A. Moss, *Plagiopodopsis cockerelliae,* Yale University specimen YPM 35484. B. Beech-like leaf (extinct genus), *Fagopsis longifolia,* Yale University specimen YPM 30121. C. Fir pollen, *Abies* cf. *venusta,* photograph by Estella Leopold from specimens USNM 50323 and USNM 50343 (Courtesy of Smithsonian Institution). D. Flower (extinct genus), *Florissantia speirii,* University of California Museum of Paleontology specimen UCMP 3619. E. Birch-like leaf (extinct genus), *Paracarpinus fraterna,* University of California Museum of Paleontology specimen UCMP 198423. F. Legume pod, *Prosopis linearifolia,* specimen UCM 8623 (Courtesy of the University of Colorado Museum of Natural History). G. Maple leaf, *Acer florissantii,* University of California Museum of Paleontology specimen UCMP 3827.

Plate 12. Fossil insects. A. Parasitic wasp, *Parabates memorialis,* specimen UCM 8575 (Courtesy of the University of Colorado Museum of Natural History). B. Leaf-rolling weevil, *Trypanorhynchus minutissimus,* specimen USNM 90587E (Courtesy of Smithsonian Institution). C. Hunting spider (extinct genus), *Palaeodrassus ingenuus,* specimen MCZ 83 (Courtesy of the Museum of Comparative Zoology, Harvard University). D. Caterpillar, *Phylledestes vorax,* specimen UCM 4608 (Courtesy of the University of Colorado Museum of Natural History). E. Caddisfly, *Derobrochus typharum,* specimen UCM 18611 (Courtesy of the University of Colorado Museum of Natural History). F. Earwig, *Labiduromma gurneyi,* specimen UCM 29920 (Courtesy of the University of Colorado Museum of Natural History). G. Tsetse fly, *Glossina oligocenus,* photograph by Dena Smith of specimen UCM 31594 (Courtesy of the University of Colorado Museum of Natural History).

Plate 13. Fossil vertebrates. A. Opossum, *Peratherium* cf. *huntii,* specimen USNM 11955 (Courtesy of Smithsonian Institution). B. Pirate Perch, *Tricophanes foliarum,* specimen FLFO 5873 (Courtesy of Florissant Fossil Beds National Monument). C. Shorebird, unidentified, specimen DMNH 50768 (Courtesy of the Denver Museum of Nature & Science).

Judge Chilson allowed me to testify for over an hour. Just before I took the stand, however, Yannacone called John Ten Eyck, a Colorado state official he had subpoenaed the day before the hearing. He asked Ten Eyck whether he was attempting to lure business and industry from other states to relocate to Colorado. When Ten Eyck acknowledged that he was employed to encourage business and industry to relocate to Colorado, Yannacone asked him whether the Florissant fossil beds were one of the natural wonders and scenic attractions he referred to in his relocation efforts. When Ten Eyck testified that the Florissant fossil beds were indeed an important natural resource the virtues of which he regularly extolled, Yannacone asked him whether he could estimate the value of a Florissant Fossil Beds National Monument to the Colorado tourist economy. Extrapolating from Dinosaur National Monument, he estimated the value of a Florissant Fossil Beds National Monument at $64 million in its first year. This was to become a critical piece of evidence on the next appeal.[6]

After I finished testifying, Yannacone made his closing statement, expecting that the defense would present its arguments next. Instead, Judge Chilson reached into his briefcase, pulled out a nine-page decision he had already prepared, and began reading. He rejected all of the Yannacone's arguments for the same reasons stated on July 9, adding acerbically that apparently Yannacone had not learned anything about the law of private property rights since his last appearance. When the judge finished reading, he denied our application for a preliminary injunction and firmly stated, "Case dismissed."[7] Immediately after the hearing, Park Land Company announced that bulldozers would begin excavation that afternoon.

The Defenders of Florissant met in the hallway. It was going to cost considerably more money, something in the neighborhood of $12,000, to appeal Judge Chilson's decision, perhaps all the way to the U.S. Supreme Court, our lawyers told us. That was just the cost of transcripts and printing the appellate briefs and Record on Appeal. The lawyers were only having their expenses covered. We definitely did not have that kind of money. Bettie and I agonized over what to do. It looked like we were finished. Then I remembered to call Vim Wright at the Colorado Springs radio station to give her the bad news— to tell her we had lost in court.

As I drove back to the U.S. Geological Survey office, depressed and worried, I turned on the radio and heard Vim's voice from Colorado Springs, talking about the case. She announced that she and her friends, accompanied by the print media, were on their way to Florissant where they would lie down in front of the bulldozers to prevent the excavation.

Not much was likely to come of it, I suspected. Dispirited, I was still sitting at my desk when the phone rang. It was Bettie Willard. "Oh, Estella! Ed Connors says he has found the money—maybe $12,000. Get back here right away! We *will* appeal!" Amazed, I jumped in my car and hurried back to meet Dick Lamm, Tom Lamm, Victor Yannacone, Roger Hansen, and Bettie at the courthouse.

Yannacone and the Lamms had already drafted an affidavit itemizing the errors that Judge Chilson had made during the previous hearings. The judge, for example, had not permitted as evidence any of the documents other than the complaint and affidavits as part of the order to show cause. Our lawyers took the additional affidavits, their legal brief, and my affidavit to the Tenth Circuit Court of Appeals for a second time.

This time, however, it was necessary first to obtain permission from the court to present the appeal and be heard. Before the panel would appeal and hear our argument for a preliminary injunction halting the bulldozers, Yannacone had to convince a single judge, Jean S. Breitenstein, of the merits of the appeal. The Tenth Circuit Court of Appeals rarely heard arguments on appeal when a preliminary injunction had been denied by the district court.

Judge Breitenstein was reluctant to grant our application and finally Yannacone argued that the uncontradicted testimony of John Ten Eyck, a Colorado state official, had established that the Florissant Fossil Beds National Monument would contribute an estimated $64 million to the economy of the State of Colorado. He reminded the judge that "[a] hundred years ago when Colorado was a Territory, if some bandit tried to steal $64 million from the people of the Territory, they would have hung the bastard, so why are we arguing about a hearing now?" Judge Breitenstein seemed somewhat startled at this. He left the bench and disappeared into the judge's chambers.

A few minutes later federal district judges Murrah, Breitenstein, and Hickey, the same three jurists who had presided over our appeal of July 10, entered the courtroom. Again in their long, black robes, they were impressive. We Defenders of Florissant were seated along with the defense lawyer Robert Johnson. The tension we all felt in that room was palpable. It was very, very quiet. Then Chief Justice Murrah asked our lawyers to present our case. It appeared that we were going to have a hearing.

This time, Yannacone expanded on our legal position by asserting, "Your honors, the Federal Courts have a duty to cooperate with Congress." By issuing a preliminary injunction pending the final deliberation of the Congress of the United States, they would be aiding the "orderly operations of the Legislative and Executive branches of government."[9] Yannacone restated his view that the Public Trust Doctrine protected the fossil beds "because the land had acquired a public character due to the recent actions of Congress."[10]

At this point Robert Johnson, attorney for the Park Land Company, argued that damage from the development would be insignificant. It certainly would not cause serious, permanent, and irreparable damage to the fossil beds because "the proposed roads would only gouge as much as 12 inches deep into the fossil sites, while each housing site would create a scar only 50 feet long and 30 or 40 feet wide." Yannacone quickly challenged Johnson, stating that this is like saying to scrape paint off the *Mona Lisa* would not do serious, irreparable damage because the canvas is still intact. Yannacone also challenged Johnson to give evidence that the defendants would lose money, as they had claimed, if the court issued a restraining order. Johnson did not reply and the defendants had provided no actual evidence to the court that they would suffer any economic damage from a temporary restraining order.[11]

The judges asked a few questions and then filed out. After a long wait we were finally told by a court assistant that the appeals court was taking our case under advisement; that is, they reserved their decision for a later time.

Bettie and I held our breath. It didn't sound good; what did this all mean? But our lawyers informed us with big smiles that in effect we had won, as it meant the earlier restraining order would be continued until that later time when and if the judges reached their decision.[12]

We suddenly became terrifically excited. Really? How wonderful! We hugged everyone over and over again. Oh my, oh my!

At the end of the hearing, Yannacone and Tom Lamm, followed by lawyer Robert Johnson, headed for the elevator up to Chief Justice Murrah's chambers on the fourth floor. All the while Johnson was hollering loudly at Yannacone, calling him every name in the book. "You son of a bitch, you Kike from New York, you Jew boy, God damn you!"[13] This went on right up to the chamber door where Tom knocked. Expecting a clerk to open the door, they were surprised to see that it was Murrah himself. The judge could not help but hear the foul language Johnson was firing at Yannacone, who, ironically, is Catholic. Murrah asked Tom Lamm (who used to clerk for one of the circuit court justices) to step into his chamber and closed the door. "Lawyer, what is going on?" asked Murrah. Lamm explained what had transpired on the way to Murrah's chambers. He added that we were now hopeful that Congress really was about to act. (The House Committee had actually released the Florissant bill for consideration, which was a first step.) Murrah then sat down at his desk and deliberately stated very clearly twice that a temporary restraining order only lasts ten days. "Lawyer, you know that," he said. Then Murrah very purposefully opened the bottom left-hand drawer of his desk and said, "Lawyer, see: I am putting the file on this case in here. You call me when this is over and Congress has acted [to create the monument]." Tom Lamm answered gratefully, "Yes, indeed, your Honor! Indeed we will."[14]

As we left the courthouse, Johnson turned to Yannacone and said, "I'm going to teach you how we practice law in white man's country. Before you can serve the order we're going to start bulldozing that road."[15]

Down on the first floor I had remembered to call my rancher friend Nate Snare at Florissant to find out what was happening at the site. I asked if he had seen the women and children that had planned to go down to the site if our earlier hearing that day with Judge Chilson hadn't gone well.

"Yeah, I saw them," said Nate. "They was carrying bedrolls as though they was going to stay the night. But they was all dressed up, so I could not figure that out. And some were carrying cameras."

"Where are they now?" I asked. "Can you give them a message?"

"Well, I can try. This is a pretty big place, you know. "

"OK, Nate, please tell them that we just won in court; tell them we won our appeal in court. Got that? Be sure to tell them."[16]

When Vim Wright's group of women returned from Florissant, they told us that they first had found the bulldozer drivers at the Thunderbird Bar in Florissant. The ladies went up to them and announced that they were going to block passage of the bulldozers. The men looked anxious and said, "Oh, you are?" But the ladies promised first to meet them in the field with a thermos of hot coffee and brandy, in case that sounded good to them. The answer was that, yes, they would share spiked coffee with the ladies at the site.

During the Florissant Fossil Beds National Monument's fortieth anniversary celebration in August 2009, I talked with Mary Burton and later with Carolyn Johnson, two of the women on Vim Wright's bulldozer team. After visiting the Thunderbird Bar, they said, they had driven to the location where the bulldozers were expected to enter the monument area.

I was fortunate to track down Holly Buchan, who as a child was a member of Wright's "team." Holly wrote:

My mother "Didda" and Mrs. Wright were friends. . . . They were very involved in historic preservation efforts in Colorado. As far back as I can remember, saving old places and old things was a value. I have a memory of being 4 or 5 years old and being swept into our station wagon by my mom, with a picnic basket for a ride to Florissant. I knew about Florissant and may have already been there before this particular trip. I was obsessed with fossils and dinosaurs. I had been impressed with how impressed my grandfather was by the big dinosaur words I could say. As a result I thought I was very smart and powerful.

At Florissant I remember meeting up with what seemed like many people we knew and many cars. Once out of the car I saw some big bulldozer-type vehicles. I remember standing and staring at them. They were big and fierce like dinosaurs. I heard my mom (behind me) saying something like "Just stand still. Don't move, Honey! They won't hurt you." I felt like I was alone there to face down/stop the bulldozers from breaking all the fossils.

Now I know that it was actually John Wright's mom who rallied the troupes and made the difference that day. My memory of this event is tiny but I have never forgotten it.[17]

For whatever reason, the bulldozers were there but the drivers never appeared. Something mysterious had happened. Much later, I learned that someone who could talk a good workman's line with the correct country twang had called and scared the hell out of those bulldozer drivers. We were not told how that came about, but something certainly had happened. We will never know.

The day after our second appeal, July 30, a wonderful cartoon by Pulitzer Prize–winning artist Pat Oliphant appeared in the *Denver Post* (figure 5.4). It showed an angry man with a mustache and black top hat sitting atop a bulldozer labeled "Developers" and gnashing his teeth. Lying on the ground in front of the bulldozer is a thin woman in high heels rolled up in a rug bearing the word "Florissant." Pat Oliphant kindly sent the original to Vim Wright at her home address in Denver. A headline appeared on July 30 in the *Coloradoan* at Fort Collins reading "Court Order Halts Construction at Monument Site."

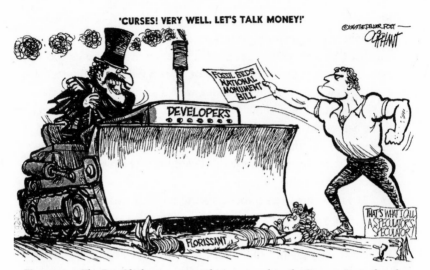

Figure 5.4. The Pat Oliphant cartoon that appeared in the Denver Post after the Vim Wright team went to Florissant on July 29, 1969, hoping to slow down the bulldozers (OLIPHANT © 1969 UNIVERSAL UCLICK. Reprinted with permission. All rights reserved.)

Acts of Congress

On July 29, before the news of our court victory that day reached Washington, D.C., the Colorado congressional delegation—Republican senators Gordon Allott and Peter Dominick, Republican representative Donald Brotzman, and Democratic representatives Wayne Aspinall, Frank Evans, and Byron Rogers—sent a strongly worded telegram to the four officers of the Park Land Company. As quoted by the August 1 *Rocky Mountain News*, the telegram in part read:

> We are informed that your organization has entered into an agreement to purchase a part of the proposed monument site, and that present plans provide for commercial development of the tract. It is our sincere belief that the Florissant lake bed is a scientific treasure house of national and even worldwide significance. As such, it would be tragic for these irreplaceable and fragile fossil remains to be disturbed or destroyed.[18]

Meanwhile, the House of Representatives appeared at last to be ready to join the Senate in moving forward on the Florissant matter. The first step had occurred on July 21, 1969, when the House Interior and Insular Affairs Committee, through its Subcommittee on Parks and Recreation, favorably and finally reported out an amended version of the Florissant Fossil Beds National Monument bill. Floor action by the House was scheduled for August 4.

Even though committee chairman Wayne Aspinall was in mourning over the loss of his mother that week, on August 4 he called on his colleagues to waive the rules and bring the bill to the full House for action as soon as possible. On the House floor, Aspinall said:

> Mr. Speaker, I rise in support of S. 912 as amended by the Committee on Interior and Insular Affairs.
>
> As most Members of the House will recall, we considered and approved legislation authorizing the establishment of the Florissant Fossil Beds National Monument during the 90th Congress. That legislation had the same objectives as S. 912 but it differed in one significant respect—that is, it authorized the acquisition of 1,000 acres of land within a designated area of 6,000 acres; whereas, S. 912 authorizes the acquisition of the 6,000 acre area. I might say at this point that the 6,000-acre national monument had the support of both the current and past administrations. . . . [I]n the judgment of the National Park Service, 6,000 acres is viewed as the minimum amount of land necessary to adequately accommodate visitors and, at the same time, achieve the preservation objectives of the area. . . . The [Senate] bill explicitly limits the amount authorized to be appropriated to $3,727,000. . . . In light of all these facts, Mr. Speaker, as chairman of the Interior and Insular Affairs Committee, I recommend enactment of S. 912.[19]

Earlier that day, after both Frank Evans and Byron Rogers spoke briefly in favor of the bill and a description of the qualities of the Florissant fossil beds had been read into the *Congressional Record*, Donald Brotzman stood anxiously before his colleagues on the House floor, defending the bill as reported from Representative Aspinall's Interior Committee on July 21. It had been a long wait for floor action. This was about the sixth such bill, give or take a few, that had been buried in Aspinall's committee since 1964.

Brotzman,[20] apparently unaware of the circuit court's continuance of the injunction four days earlier, or choosing to ignore it for dramatic effect, told the House:

[E]ven though this priceless window into the Oligocene [*sic*] period has lain undisturbed for 34 million years now, its destruction could come this very afternoon. . . . Early in July a coalition of citizen groups, fighting to preserve Florissant, won a temporary restraining order against a major Colorado Springs developer which plans to build A-frame vacation cabins on the site, prompting the remark "to build A-frames on this singular, national resource would be like wrapping fish in the Dead Sea Scrolls." That order has expired and the builder has announced plans to bulldoze his access road through the fossil beds today.

Brotzman continued:

In the light of the clear and present danger to this unique open-air museum, the House Interior Committee, at the direction of my distinguished colleague (Mr. ASPINALL), agreed to seek a suspension of the rules to bring this bill, S. 912, to create the Florissant Fossil Beds National Monument before the House.

Mr. Speaker, I would urge my colleagues to take this opportunity to prevent the destruction of a national treasure. Preserving the Florissant today will be relatively easy, but even 24 hours from now it may be futile.

The House of Representatives did act—and quickly. They voted to bypass Rules Committee review of the bill after Wayne Aspinall termed it a measure of historical importance, triggering a voice vote that very day. One legislator was notorious for blocking any voice vote, which must be unanimously approved, by voicing his opposition on principle. But two friendly colleagues hovered over this fellow during the vote on Florissant so that he could not put in his "Nay." With that, the bill sailed unanimously through the House. Florissant legislation had finally passed both houses of the Congress in some form.

The bill then went back to the Senate for approval of the House amendments. The Senate voted their final approval with a voice vote three days later, on August 7. The measure was flown by special courier plane on August 14, with other approved measures, to the summer White House in San Clemente, California, where it was signed into law by President Richard Nixon on August 20, 1969 (Public Law 91-60).

What excitement prevailed at the board meeting of the Colorado Open Space Coordinating Council later that month! There was "dancing in the halls!" We just crowed with delight at our success. It felt so good that we as citizens had worked together and had added our weight to the deliberations, influencing the American process of government. We cheered for the local, state, and national branches of government that had contributed to saving the fossil beds. We sent up big hurrahs for our lawyers, the grand bandleaders who conducted the action, and of course, for our esteemed appeals court justices. Tom Lamm later called Alfred Murrah to inform him that Congress had acted to pass the bill and President Nixon had signed it. Murrah—still holding the appellate papers in his desk—replied, "Well, lawyer, then I am sorry to tell you that you have lost your appeal." It was the best "loss" Tom Lamm ever had.[21]

Despite the judicial and legislative victories, the Defenders of Florissant still had work to do raising funds. Joanne Ditmar of the *Denver Post* issued an appeal for funds on behalf of the Defenders of Florissant in her column, while Vim Wright and Ed Connors solicited donations from their Rocky Mountain friends. As a result, more than $12,000 was raised and the group was able to pay its bills.

Ironically, in the end, it may have been the single-minded development pressure from the Park Land Company that was a deciding factor in pushing Congress to act. Even so, it was the innovative action of our lawyers in designing a winning strategy that kept the land safe while Congress pondered. The broad spectrum of ongoing public support, informed by consistent coverage from the media, also made a really important difference. Public pressure for preservation had built steadily from the early 1960s through the end of the decade. The experience we gained participating in this fight brought recognition and strength to the budding environmental movement in Colorado and to the Colorado Open Space Council.

At the end of the long summer of 1969, the saga of saving the Florissant fossil beds for federal protection was over. The threat of a geologic "book burning" was extinguished. The Florissant Fossil Beds National Monument was established for future generations to study and enjoy. Finally, the door was open for the National Park Service to move in.

Chapter Six

The National Park Service Steps In

۱۷

HERBERT W. MEYER

THE NATIONAL PARK SERVICE FACED A VARIETY OF CHALLENGES WHEN it came to developing the new monument. First, the land had to be purchased and brought under a single coherent plan for its management. This management needed to provide an educational experience for the growing number of visitors that were expected to arrive. The interpretive explanation of the fossil beds required credible, coherent science, and this could only be accomplished by supporting a paleontology research program. It took many years before some of these objectives were achieved, and some, even still, are but dreams.

Buying the Land

Even though Congress had passed the legislation to create Florissant Fossil Beds National Monument and President Nixon had signed it into law, actually buying the land from the private property holders took several years to accomplish. Congress had appropriated $3.72 million for the purchase of 6,000 acres and for necessary development expenses. The monument's size was defined by that original legislation and has not increased since (figure 6.1). In total, eighteen tracts of land, including a variety of buildings, were acquired from fourteen owners to achieve the monument's authorized maximum area (figure 6.2; table 6.1).[1]

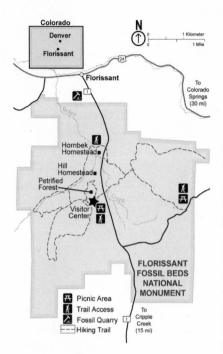

Figure 6.1. Map of Florissant Fossil Beds National Monument. (Map drafted by Lindsay Walker; courtesy of Florissant Fossil Beds National Monument.)

The creation of a national monument out of privately owned land was unusual and it was not always easy to determine what the fair market value should be. The Wells family, whose land was located both inside and outside the monument's planned boundaries, decided that the only way to determine fair value was to sell a parcel that lay outside the proposed boundary and use that sale as a guide to the value of their land inside the monument.[2] Some landowners simply felt they were not adequately compensated by the price they received. The Singer family, for example, felt that their property had been undervalued though they were very much in favor of the monument. At times, more than simple compensation was at stake, and some landowners had difficulty accepting the idea of leaving their homes. As one property

Figure 6.2 Map showing tracts of private land that were acquired to form Florissant Fossil Beds National Monument. The petrified forest properties were owned by the Baker (label 8) and Singer (label 4) families. See table 6.1 for a key and detailed description. Based on the National Park Service Division of Land Acquisition map of Florissant Fossil Beds National Monument, compiled in August 1969 from basic land ownership data of March 1967. (Map drafted by Christina Whitmore; courtesy of Florissant Fossil Beds National Monument.)

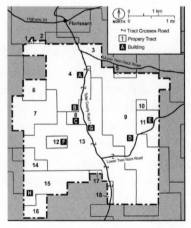

Table 6.1. Tracts of private land acquired to form Florissant Fossil Beds National Monument

Map label in Figure 6.2	Tract number	Owner	Acreage	Buildings	Purchase price
1	01-115	Kenneth Fallis	15		$5,000
2	01-116	Park Land Company	15		*
3	01-117	A. W. Gregg	80.40		$20,000
4	01-102	A. R. Singer	864 ±	A - Singer bunkhouse (later developed by the NPS into the "Hornbek Homestead" theme attraction). B - Colorado Petrified Forest Lodge (later demolished by the NPS).	$475,000
5	01-114	Danford Barney	40.83		$10,000
6	01-112	Mary Kelly	160		$20,000
7	01-121	W. Nate Snare	440		**
8	01-101	John Baker	73 ±	C - Pike Petrified Forest building (later developed into the NPS visitor center and demolished in 2011)	$235,000
9	01-118	Park Land Company	1,630.09	D - Cusack potato barn	*
10	01-113	Max Ewald	40		$5,400
11	01-111	Delbert T. Wells	200	E - Wells' cabin and outbuildings (some later moved for use at Hornbek theme attraction)	$125,000
12	01-107	Ione Jones	80	F - A-frame cabin (later developed as education facility and paleontology laboratory)	***
13	01-103	John Maytag	1,624 ±	G - Maytag barn (later used as an NPS maintenance center)	$310,000
14	01-106	Ione Jones	120		***
15	01-108	Mathilde Nelson	440	H - Nelson log cabin (later moved off-site), "white house," and outbuildings	$80,000
16	01-109	Walter Witcher	120		$54,000
17	01-100	W. Nate Snare	10		**
18	01-105	W. Nate Snare	40		**

Source: Land data based on National Park Service Division of Land Acquisition map of Florissant Fossil Beds National Monument, compiled in August 1969 from basic land ownership data of March 1967, FLFO-6906, Florissant Fossil Beds National Monument Archive, Colorado. Prices of land sales from C. Given and W. Stark, Land History of Florissant Fossil Beds National Monument, unpublished report, May 2000, FLFO-423, Florissant Fossil Beds National Monument Archive, Colorado.

*Tracts 2 and 9 were purchased for a total of $345,000.

**Tracts 7, 17, and 18 were purchased for a total of $205,000.

***Tracts 12 and 14 were purchased for a total of $52,400.

owner later commented, eminent domain is a good idea until it is your home.[3] One of the first rangers at Florissant even felt a sense of melancholy for the people who had to leave the land they had called home for so long.[4]

Purchasing the Pike Petrified Forest from John Baker was a particularly lengthy challenge. Baker filed a complaint about condemnation on that tract of land in 1970, with a trial eventually set for July 1974. Just days before the trial was scheduled to begin, the judge postponed it indefinitely. Baker then brought in a front loader and started digging holes of various sizes all over his property. Such destructive action was apparently an attempt to determine how many fossil stumps still lay buried.[5] This final threat to the fossil beds prompted the Park Service to file a suit to take immediate possession of the property, and a federal court granted title to the United States on November 5, 1974. This transfer finally opened the door for the Park Service to renovate Baker's old Pike Petrified Forest building and begin operating it as a visitor center.

Once they had been purchased, the various parcels of land needed to be integrated to begin the design and operation of the new monument. One of the consequences of piecemeal amalgamation of land to create a monument is in certain circumstances having to grant easements. Even today, there remain instances in which the monument must honor the right of adjacent landowners to cross monument land if that is the only reasonable route to reach their property.

Ranch Tails and Fossil Dogs

The legislation that created the new monument clearly defined its purpose: "to preserve and interpret for the benefit and enjoyment of present and future generations the excellently preserved insect and leaf fossils and related geologic sites and objects at the Florissant lakebeds."[6] Fulfilling this mandate involves preservation and protection of fossil resources, ongoing scientific research, and education and interpretation for visitors.

During its formative years, policies for the fledgling monument were being steered in directions divergent from its purpose, in part as an attempt to attract more tourists and local visitors. Even as some of the petrified trees were being reburied "so they would not be obvious" to visitors who might chip away at them, new aspects of the human history of the area were being revealed and given some prominence.[7] The thought behind this was that visitors might find displays on the recent human past more attractive than those about what the world was like more than 30 million years ago.

The Park Service discovered that an old house on the Singer property was the site of an early homestead.[8] Among the people living in the valley during the settlement period was Adeline Hornbek, the first person to officially file a homestead claim in the area in 1878. Widowed by her first husband and separated from her second, Adeline lived near Florissant with her four children, and her story has been used by the Park Service to demonstrate a woman's pioneering spirit and independence.

The Hornbek Homestead was placed on the National Register of Historic Places in 1981, and the house has become one of the monument's interpretive highlights. Twice a year, the interior of the house opens to the public, staffed by local volunteers in period clothing and filled with aromas of baking bread and apple pie, alluring even to a paleontologist. The Park Service has moved old buildings from other locations around the monument to the site to create a replica of an old homestead. It seems an ironic twist that Walt Disney purchased a petrified stump from Florissant that eventually was displayed at Frontierland, the historic theme park at Disneyland, while years later the National Park Service focused on creating its own "frontierland" homestead replica within the petrified forest itself.

During the 1970s, as Hornbek was emerging as a new-found figure in local history, her former neighbors, Charlotte and Adam Hill, had been forgotten. Charlotte Hill's fossil discoveries included the world's finest fossil butterfly (see figure 1.2), and her contacts with early paleontologists had contributed significantly to making Florissant world famous. The Hills were rarely mentioned in the history presented to monument visitors, in part simply because their old house no longer stood. Another irony was that the Hill house, built by Adam Hill in 1874, was the only one in the vicinity shown on the 1878 map by Arthur Lakes, the geologist who accompanied Samuel Scudder. An early newspaper, the *Fairplay Flume*, reported in 1880 that Charlotte Hill, who was then thirty-one years old with four children, had taken particular pride in the fossils and had become a self-made naturalist and collector.[9] She "displayed at her home an elegant array of geological specimens" and collected a huge number of the specimens that were used to describe dozens of new species of fossils, three of which were named for her, including a fossil rose. Of the 120 plant species that were originally named by Leo Lesquereux alone, at least a third—and probably many more—were based on specimens Charlotte Hill had collected. Although she was the homesteader whose contributions had had such an important impact on Florissant's rise to world fame, her story was neglected as history instead was spun around the standing Hornbek house.

By the late 1970s, the monument's growing emphasis on the area's cultural history and focus on the Hornbek Homestead was beginning to draw attention and resources away from its real purpose, the preservation and presentation of the fossils. The trend drew pointed criticism from, among others, Harry MacGinitie in 1979 during his last visit to Florissant—and his first since he had testified ten years earlier before the Senate subcommittee hearing in Colorado Springs (figure 6.3). He was eighty-three years old and was returning with the invitation and support of the National Park Service.

MacGinitie moved slowly, grasping a stout tree branch for a walking stick as he revisited some of his old collecting sites and the campsite where he had stayed forty-two years earlier. Asked during an interview with the Park Service for his opinion of the monument's attention to the old homestead building, he

responded emphatically: "The cultural history of the immediate area should be rather brief. I mean, it shouldn't be too important. The fundamental thing about this place is the fossils! . . . That's the name of the monument! From what I see here, when that [historical interpretive plan] is completed, that's enough! No more. No more. Let's not go off on a tangent on the history. It's [a story] repeated in a hundred places up and down the Rockies, the same thing as we have at Mrs. Hornbek's place. I don't think it should be emphasized too much."[10]

This "pull of the recent" is a problem that other paleontology parks face, too. A former director of the National Park Service once referred to it as the historic ranch tail wagging the fossil dog. Even today, Park Service managers—constantly swayed by changing bureaucratic

Figure 6.3. Harry D. MacGinitie during his visit to Florissant in 1979. (Courtesy of Florissant Fossil Beds National Monument.)

trends, and by costly diversions ranging from restoration of old buildings to eradication of exotic weeds—still need to be reminded from time to time why paleontology parks are designated in the first place. The important story to be told at Florissant is what the fossils tell us about changes on Earth through time, MacGinitie stressed.

The Promise of Paleontology

In a 1969 letter from the office of the secretary of the Interior to Senator Henry M. "Scoop" Jackson, chair of the Senate Committee on Interior and Insular Affairs, the department clearly indicated that a paleontologist was to be hired during the first year of the new monument's operation, followed in subsequent years by rangers and caretakers.[11] This intention was specifically reaffirmed by Congress.[12] The priority to implement this position from the moment of the monument's creation would help fulfill the congressionally defined purpose, "to assure that a significant portion of this resource remains available for future scientific explorations," and that this scientific research would enable the layman to understand the significance of the fossils.[13] But the good intentions floundered, and it was not until twenty-five years later that the National Park Service finally created a permanent paleontology position to begin focusing on the monument's real purpose.

Developing a program to protect and research the fossils was clearly vital to the monument's mission. New excavations could not begin without staff expertise in paleontology. Developing exhibits and interpretation required synthesizing a huge amount of previous research into readily understood terms. Moreover, ongoing research is crucial for unraveling new knowledge about Florissant's ancient secrets.

In the absence of a paleontologist on staff, some of the first paleontological work the monument sponsored was conducted by an elderly volunteer, F. Martin Brown, one of the founders of the Fountain Valley School near Colorado Springs. He had been interested in the Florissant fossil insects since 1931 and published several short papers on the subject during the years he volunteered, including the descriptions for two new species of fossil butterflies.[14] Finally, in 1992, a seasonal paleontology position was funded for two seasons, and in 1994, I (Herb Meyer) accepted the monument's first permanent paleontology position.

Recollections of a Monument Paleontologist

My interest in coming to Florissant stemmed mainly from a long fascination with fossil floras of the Eocene and Oligocene epochs. I still recall the day when one of my early mentors, Jack Wolfe, gave me a copy of MacGinitie's monograph on the *Fossil Plants of the Florissant Beds*.[15] I was a junior in high school at the time, working on a project to describe a fossil plant site in Oregon,[16] and

Wolfe, a world-renowned paleobotanist with the U.S. Geological Survey and a colleague of Estella Leopold, had taken on the role of my advisor. With a suitcase full of these fossils in hand, I took the bus from Oregon to California to meet with him. When he gave me the copy of MacGinitie's Florissant monograph, I remember asking him, "Florissant, where's that?"

Many years later, in August 1994, having long since learned of Florissant's importance and included it in my doctoral research,[17] I began work as the monument's paleontologist. Less than two weeks later, the monument celebrated its twenty-fifth anniversary. This made it a festive time to begin and a good time to meet many of the people who had played such important roles in the monument's history (plate 4). Just three months later, the monument sponsored a conference in Colorado Springs called Partners in Paleontology, bringing together many organizations that shared the goal of protecting and understanding fossil resources.[18] Florissant was emerging as a leading site in fossil resource protection and scientific research.

One of the first projects I initiated was to pull together all of the information about the Florissant fossils that had been collected and described by the early paleontologists—which turned out to be much more than anyone expected. These research collections had gone decades earlier to museums throughout the world and remained in their ownership. With Park Service funding, in 1995 I traveled to the Smithsonian's National Museum of Natural History in Washington, D.C., the first of seventeen museums I was to visit and the location of the largest collection of Florissant fossils. It took the equivalent of a full year's worth of time—spread over eight years—just to get through all of these collections and photograph them. And that was only time enough to see the five thousand fossils that had actually been included in previous publications. The remaining thirty-five thousand or more unpublished specimens were too much to include.

In 1996 I made my first visit to see Samuel Scudder's collections of insects and spiders at Harvard. Cabinets were filled with treasures such as the butterfly *Prodryas persephone* that Charlotte Hill had found more than 125 years before (see figure 1.2). *Prodryas* rests in a little customized cedar box with a sliding lid, embedded in plaster, and it is one of the museum's most priceless fossils. Drawers upon drawers were filled with tiny insect fossils, so many that it would take months to go through them all. This, more than anything else, made me appreciate just how enormous Scudder's work at Florissant had been. After all, I was just there to take photographs and record information, which took only a few months to finish. Scudder had actually labored for years to describe, name, and illustrate each and every one of them.

Returning from one of these museums visits, I gazed out the window of the plane, wondering how to make all of this information more accessible to the public. It was already our intention to create a database on the Internet (completed in 2002), but I wanted to reach a broader audience. Very few Florissant fossils were on exhibit anywhere, and for the first time, information on the entirety of Florissant's fossil wealth was coming together in one place, and I had pictures—thousands of pictures! By the time the plane landed in Colorado Springs, the idea for a book, *The Fossils of Florissant*, had become an ambition for me. It was finally published six years later.[19] In addition, funding from the National Park Service later made it possible to create the database and website that now makes this information publicly accessible.[20]

Another big project was to start new excavations (figure 6.4) that were needed to gather new data for testing research hypotheses, because many of the older collections never documented precise collecting locations or the geologic context. As a result of these excavations, the monument's collection of fossils grew from 631 specimens in 1994 to more than 10,000 by the end of 2011. Actually finding the spectacular fossils at Florissant is no easy task. In 1916, T. D. A. Cockerell noted that "those who have seen the exhibits in museums are likely to be disappointed when visiting the locality, since first class specimens are few, and it often seems that nothing of value is being obtained to compensate for the labor in cramped and uncomfortable positions. Yet, in the hands of experts, the yield is such that it would be hard to duplicate elsewhere."[21] MacGinite, too, remarked that at

Figure 6.4. Paleontology staff and interns work with the monument's paleontologist Herb Meyer to excavate fossils. (Courtesy of Dena Smith.)

Florissant "more labor is required to obtain a given number of specimens than at any other fossil plant locality."[22] It takes a lot of patience—and splitting many pieces of shale—before the fruits of these labors reveal new discoveries. Yet the lure of new discoveries is exciting, and new, unknown pieces of the ancient puzzle continue to emerge. For instance, in 2008, Florissant's first fossil *Ginkgo* leaf was revealed.

Most of these projects would not have been possible without the help of interns (figure 6.5). Beginning in 1997, the monument began a long-term program of sponsoring paleontology interns during the summer. Since then, more than thirty paleontology interns have made tremendous contributions to a large variety of projects—monitoring and photographing all of the fossil sites in the monument, assisting with research and excavations, and creating new databases and websites about the fossils. Several interns have gone on to write theses and publish papers on Florissant's paleontology. April Kinchloe, for example, was but one of these many ambitious interns. She arrived at the end of her junior year in the summer of 1998 and returned almost every year for the next seven either as an intern or a student member of the paleontology staff. She worked to build the fossil database, excavate fossils and catalog them for the monument's collection, and later complete a thesis on the fossil spiders.[23]

One of the greatest benefits in having Florissant managed as a national monument is the support by the National Park Service for funding special projects in paleontology. Some of the funding comes from the entry fees that visitors pay, and a portion of that money is used to support new research. This

Figure 6.5. Student interns work with the monument's paleontologist and play an important role in preparing and cataloging fossils for the monument's collections. (Courtesy of Dena Smith.)

research, in turn, enables the monument to provide scientifically credible information for interpreting the fossils to the public. These projects have included not only new excavations at Florissant, but also research at other locations where new knowledge helps to place the Florissant fossils in a broader context. Together with Estella Leopold and a group of scientists from the University of Arizona, for example, we examined modern forests in northeastern Mexico as a means for better understanding the ancient plant community at Florissant. Other projects have focused specifically on the preservation of the fossils, including new investigations of strategies for stabilizing the fossil stumps, and annual monitoring of the condition of the fossil sites. Another funded project has supported the completion of this book.

A Natural Attraction for Scientists

A news release by the Defenders of Florissant in 1969 described Florissant as "a marvelous place to visit, for the tourist or the professional."[24] Florissant is a natural laboratory for scientists, especially paleontologists and geologists. The National Monument serves to entice the public's interest in fossils, but it is the scientific research of these fossils that gives them meaning. Scientists from around the world come to Florissant, some on professional field trips and others to conduct studies that will expand our knowledge of the ancient past.

Visiting researchers from different universities bring innovative ideas for looking at Florissant's fossils and have often advanced scientific understanding of the ancient Florissant world in their work. With approved research permits, they are able to dig in the monument in their search for answers to scientific questions. Some of their conclusions have been remarkable. Dena Smith, now a professor at the University of Colorado, first came to Florissant as a graduate student from the University of Arizona, and her dissertation unveiled new ideas about how plants and insects had coevolved. It turns out that all of those little holes on the leaves—bite marks of insects— reveal some big stories. In addition, her students' work, including April Kinchloe's thesis on the spiders, has ranged from climate interpretation and preservation of fossil insects to examination of fossil diatoms.

Jaelyn Eberle and her students, also from the University of Colorado, have tripled the number of fossil mammals known from Florissant by carefully screening the sediments to find the tiny bones and teeth of rodents, rabbits, moles, and other small mammals.[25] Neal O'Brien from the State University of New York has looked at the shale with a scanning electron microscope to discover that microscopic diatoms may have been responsible for secreting a slimy mat that helped to preserve the fossil insects.

Besides those who come for research, many other scientists visit Florissant on organized field trips. Such trips are led by experts who have done research at Florissant, and they provide information to help other scientists understand Florissant's significance. Many of the participants are professors who go back to their classrooms and incorporate examples from Florissant in their teaching, and some even return with their students on university-sponsored field trips.

Professional organizations such as the Geological Society of America (GSA) play important roles at Florissant by sponsoring field trips, symposia, and interns. I led five field trips for GSA between 1996 and 2010, and another was led in 1994 by the expert on Florissant's stratigraphy, Emmett Evanoff. Estella Leopold was one of the leaders for a 1973 trip by the First International Congress of Systematic and Evolutionary Biology, which included European and Russian participants. A field trip by the International Organisation of Palaeobotany in 1996 included an impressive turnout of forty-eight paleobotanists from fifteen countries on five continents. Not all of the participants on these various trips were specialists in paleontology—one of them on my 2010 GSA trip was an Apollo astronaut who made the first flight around the Moon.

Interpreting the Fossils for the Public

Visitors to Florissant come from around the world and represent a diversity of backgrounds, interests, and ages. More than 2 million people have come to see the fossil beds since the monument was established. Those numbers grew slowly at first. The official record for the number of visitors shows twenty thousand in 1973.[26] By the 1990s, some years saw the number reach one hundred thousand, but it has dwindled in recent years to about sixty thousand annually, probably due in part to the global economic downturn. The monument's proximity to large population centers such as Colorado Springs and Denver serves as a magnet for attracting local visitors and makes it possible for various school districts to bring up to four thousand students to Florissant every year. In addition, with the expansion of the Internet, many people make virtual visits to discover Florissant's fossils on the monument's websites. One of the monument's primary functions is to interpret the fossils in a way that makes them understandable to all of these visitors.

Because the monument's primary attraction is the petrified forest adjacent to the visitor center, most visitors are able to talk with one of the interpretive rangers if they care to do so. Providing an eclectic mix of science and ranger lore, these rangers, assisted by volunteers, are the tour guides who tell stories about the significance of Florissant.

Exhibits provide one of the important means of informing visitors about the significance of Florissant. For more than thirty years, the primary exhibit at Florissant was a simple display of fossils that took up much of one wall. Although many of the fossils were impressive by themselves, they still lacked any meaningful, informative discussion. Because the national monument's fossil collections were very small before the inception of a paleontology program in 1994, many of the first specimens on exhibit had been generously loaned by Waynesburg College of Pennsylvania, which operated its summer geology field camp at Florissant for many years. Other displays in the visitor center looked more like projects from a high school science fair than exhibits appropriate for a national monument.

Beginning in 2007, several new exhibits were installed in the visitor center, followed by new wayside exhibits for the trails. These exhibits address more substantive interpretive themes that give meaning to the fossils and illustrate what they can tell us about changes in Earth's systems over time. A new interpretive excavation was developed in the late 1990s at the site of the old Singer Ranch's fossil-collecting trench. This interpretive site fulfills MacGinitie's dream of being able to demonstrate for the tourists how the fossil leaves and insects are found in a geologic context and how this landscape has changed over the immensity of geologic time. The excavation exposes fresh shale and allows monument visitors to see how the fossils occur naturally in the ground, how research data are gathered during the process of collecting, and how the shale is split apart, perhaps revealing a fossil for the first time in 34 million years.

Prompted by the preparation of this book, Charlotte Hill has also finally become a part of the national monument's interpretive story. On February 15, 2009, on the occasion of what would have been Hill's 160th birthday, a special event was held to recognize her legacy at Florissant, and a new wayside exhibit panel now tells her story. Like the women who followed almost a century later in the movement to create the national monument, Charlotte Hill is now also remembered as one Florissant's heroines.

Protecting the Fossils

Despite the fossil beds' designation as a national monument, the problem of fossils disappearing in the hands of tourists has never completely gone away. The amount of petrified wood that remains on the surface is certainly less than it was in the late 1800s, when vandalism and casual collecting began to run rampant. There is simply not as much to take away anymore. Even so, some visitors just can't resist the temptation to grab a little souvenir. The scale of such removals at Florissant is nothing like it is at other fossil parks, such as the Petrified Forest in Arizona, but on a small scale, the problem remains.

The message of protection is strongly conveyed to park visitors, but those who choose to ignore it are subject to substantial fines. Confronted by rangers who have watched them fill their pockets with pieces of petrified wood, some visitors will still stand in defiant denial of their own deeds. Even scout leaders have led their troops, and professors their classes, in pursuit of illegally collecting fossils from the shale. They violate not only the law, but also the spirit of the efforts that went into establishing Florissant as a national monument. Some people feel guilty and later contact the park to ask if they can return fossils that they collected, but without the geologic context, those fossils can have little significance.

The Long Wait for a Visitor Center

In the action to create Florissant Fossil Beds National Monument, Senators Allott and Dominick had stated several times that they wanted to pass the bill to purchase the land, but knowing the budget shortage, they realized that the buildings should come later. The first visitor center and office in 1970 was no more than a large camper trailer. The Park Service considered renovating either the old Colorado Petrified Forest Lodge or the Pike Petrified Forest building into a visitor center. In the mid-1970s, the decision was made to tear down the lodge—the same building that had been the old train station in Florissant years earlier—which was an unfortunate decision that outraged some of the local citizens. However, the expense of maintaining the old building was thought to be too high. During the decades that followed, through 2011, the old Pike Petrified Forest building served as the visitor center while the Park Service awaited funds for the construction of a new facility.

For more than forty years, the lack of a modern visitor center at Florissant was in stark contrast to what visitors were accustomed to finding at most national park units. For decades, Park Service planners promised that a new visitor center was only a couple of years away, but time after time these plans were dashed. The need for such a facility to exhibit and interpret the fossils and provide research space and collection storage was envisioned from the outset of the monument's creation.

Over the years, enormous resources and planning went into architectural designs for one visitor center after another, yet nothing ever progressed any further than paper. Shrinking budgets and a lack of continuity due to frequently changing superintendents made it difficult to bring any of these plans to fruition. The Pike Petrified Forest building, originally built by Henderson nearly fifty years before the monument's establishment, continued to serve the needs of the monument's visitors even as it slowly deteriorated.

Finally, by 2011, a pending architectural plan moved quickly through the budgetary process. On November 28, 2011, in only an hour, the old Henderson building was torn down to make way for the construction of an innovative, energy-efficient building that would serve as a visitor center and paleontology research lab. This center will provide storage for the monument's growing research collections as well as exhibit space for new displays about Florissant's fossil history. As this book goes to press, the new building is under construction.

The Value of Good Friends

One of the monument's strongest allies has been its nonprofit supporting organization, The Friends of the Florissant Fossil Beds, Inc., established in 1987. Friends groups are commonly formed by local citizens to support the mission of national parks and monuments, and they work closely with the parks to fulfill needs that might otherwise be difficult to administer.

The Friends of Florissant have been particularly active. They raise funds through membership fees, selling T-shirts, soliciting donations from other organizations, and admission fees for special events. They sponsor a seminar series during the summer, offering up to twelve accredited courses every year. These courses are designed primarily for teachers and cover topics in paleontology, geology, biology, history, and archaeology. The Friends also sponsor special events, such as monument anniversaries, field trips led by prominent scientists, and public programs in nearby cities. In collaboration

with the monument's international efforts to support research and conservation of paleontological resources abroad, the Friends of Florissant have
entered into a partnership with a Peruvian nonprofit organization dedicated
to the Piedra Chamana Petrified Forest in Sexi, Peru, supporting ongoing
efforts to conserve and study that site. They have also given support for the
completion of this book.

The Past Is the Key to the Future

During his visit to Florissant in 1979, Harry MacGinitie made a casual com-
ment that has profound implications: "We get all tangled up with the present.
The present is just a little flick in time between the past and the future. . . . We
are just in this particular little time interval, and it seems so important to us.
But . . . paleontology helps us to see at least what's gone on in the past. It does
[thereby] help solve some problems in the present."[27]

The "problems of the present" to which MacGinitie referred become
clearer as the evidence of current global climate change mounts, demon-
strating and confirming that we live on a dynamic and changeable planet.
From what it tells us about a significant climatic change 33 to 34 million years
ago—one of the biggest such changes in the past 65 million years—Florissant
helps provide us with hindsight for understanding major climate change in
our modern world. Florissant helps to show how organisms and forest ecosystems responded to major global cooling following the close of the Eocene,
and from that knowledge we can begin to realize how modern-day climate
change might affect life on Earth in the future.

The effort to understand the deep past at Florissant will never be finished. Advances in scientific techniques always hold the promise of revealing
new secrets about this ancient world. Countless pages of Florissant's paper
shale remain unturned. These pieces of shale are like lottery tickets, each
holding the possibility of being a big winner that reveals a new unknown
character from the past. It was the battle to create Florissant Fossil Beds
National Monument in 1969 that assured that scientists can continue to
unravel new secrets well into the future and that these fossil treasures will
continue to be available for all to see.

Chapter Seven

Beyond Florissant

❦

ESTELLA B. LEOPOLD AND JOHN STANSFIELD

DURING THE LATE 1960S AND THROUGH THE EARLY 1970S, A WAVE OF change swept like a tsunami across the United States and the world, bringing a better understanding of the importance of healthy environments and the need to protect natural resources. The campaign to save the Florissant fossil beds was a link in the chain that helped bring about that understanding. Issues significant in the Florissant battle—organizing local, statewide, and national public support; balancing private property rights with public values; establishing new legal precedents; the impact of the media on public policy; the roles of science, scientists, and conservation organizations in government decision making—all contributed to the development of the "environmental movement."

The skills that came to be known as grassroots organizing evolved from the labor and civil rights struggles of the nineteenth and twentieth centuries. Successful grassroots organizing requires effective communication—simple listening and speaking. As Cesar Chavez, who organized the United Farm Workers, once said, "The only way I know how to organize people is to talk to one person, then talk to another person, then talk to another person."[1]

One hundred years before the environmental movement, the communication and education process about Florissant began with curious local collectors and with international scientists who glorified the deposits by writing about them. With beautiful graphics, paleontologists portrayed the diversity—the stunning array of plants, insects, and other animals—of the Florissant ecosystem. Their writings pointed to the significance of the fossil beds in building, both for the scientific community and the general population, a fundamental understanding of the bedrock concepts of geologic time and evolutionary succession and their scientific and cultural significance.

The sometimes conflicting hopes, plans, and anxieties of ranchers, owners of the petrified forests, land developers, and conservationists brought the fate of the fossil beds to the attention of the world during the second half of the twentieth century. To address their concerns, the Defenders of Florissant hastily developed and effectively implemented a successful grassroots organizing plan. Ultimately, the campaign involved people from every level of government: town, county, state, and federal legislators; the courts; government agencies; and, finally, President Richard Nixon. All this happened so that the National Park Service could take care of the fossil beds, a desire landowner Agnes Singer expressed when she said, "It was my husband's dream to have it become part of the National Park system and come under the protection of the Rangers."

A Common Law for Natural Resources

The legal history of Florissant Fossil Beds National Monument is, in many important respects, a benchmark in U.S. environmental and constitutional law. Prior to the late 1960s, there had been a number of environmental "battles," such as with various national parks, the Cross-Florida Barge Canal, and dam proposals in Dinosaur National Monument and Grand Canyon, which stirred action in the courts and debate in public and in Congress. Nevertheless, the Florissant case came early in the course of environmental lawsuits. The case was dramatic, daring, and unprecedented.

The battle for Florissant quickly followed Victor Yannacone's successful attack in Wisconsin state court on the widespread use of persistent chlorinated chemical biocides, particularly DDT,[2] and his involvement in the creation of the Environmental Defense Fund together with a number of concerned scientists and conservationists. It preceded the National Environmental Policy Act. Earlier appeals to federal courts to protect environmental values met with little or no success. The Florissant fossil beds litigation was the first real "winner" in the struggle to establish a public right to protection of unique national natural resources.

At the same time Congress was considering the Florissant Fossil Beds National Monument bill in 1969, it was also considering legislation to establish a National Environmental Policy Act (NEPA), which eventually became law on January 1, 1970. As Victor Yannacone stated in 1975, NEPA "is more than a statement of what we believe as a people and as a nation. It established priorities and gives expression to our national goals and aspirations."[3] Under NEPA, government agencies are required to seek input from the public about the impacts of proposed actions.

The Florissant issue was developing for several years before the first Earth Day in April 1970, recognized as the premier event of the American environmental movement. In the summer of 1969, there was no national army of lawyers to defend Florissant. Even Yannacone's pioneering organization, the Environmental Defense Fund, was not interested in protecting the fossils.

Yannacone, with the help of Richard and Tom Lamm and Roger Hansen, alone opened the door to the courthouse for the Defenders of Florissant. They went forward with legal arguments that had not been heard in the courts perhaps since Cicero presented them at the height of the Roman republic; arguments from the "natural law" and the fundamental principles of equity jurisprudence, which eventually became the foundation of English common law and came to America with the Founding Fathers. Without such innovative legal arguments, the Florissant fossil beds might have been lost forever to development (plate 5).

When they were needed, the Defenders of Florissant and the American people found thoughtful and courageous jurists such as Chief Justice Alfred P.

Murrah (figure 7.1) and the other members of the U.S. Court of Appeals for the Tenth Circuit. The judges listened and recognized the larger issues at stake in the claims that the Florissant fossil beds were "a unique national natural resource treasure that

Figure 7.1. Chief Justice Alfred P. Murrah of the U.S. Circuit Court of Appeals for the Tenth Circuit. Without his leadership and understanding, the Florissant case might well have been lost to real estate developers. (Courtesy of Oklahoma Heritage Association.)

called for wise use and protection for the benefit, use and enjoyment of generations yet unborn," even where there was little substantive legal precedent for
such a case.[4]

Murrah, for whom the Oklahoma City federal building destroyed by
terrorist bombing was named, was a particular hero in this case. The
Defenders of Florissant were incredibly fortunate to have him on their appeal
hearing. He had a well-established reputation for his opinions that emphasized consideration of fundamental fairness. He emphasized qualities of legislation "founded upon justice and equity, generated . . . to right a wrong and
. . . not unconstitutional."[5] Murrah proceeded from the premise that cases
should be decided on their merits, not on technicalities.[6] Some of his cases
illustrated his insistence that litigants should have their right to a full hearing on the merits of a case.[7] Each of these themes is reminiscent of our failed
attempts to get a favorable hearing from Judge G. Hatfield Chilson.

Murrah's friendship with William O. Douglas, the great conservationist
judge, may have provided the Defenders with an advantage in their attempts
to save a great natural resource. Justice Douglas and Justice Murrah became
good friends in the 1940s and exchanged letters thereafter. Both men shared
a love of the outdoors, and fishing figured prominently in their letters.[8]

Private Ownership Versus Public Property

At the heart of the conflict in the battle to protect the fossil beds was the clash
between private property rights that included the right to destroy the fossil
beds and the public right to conserve this national treasure and landscape for
future generations (figure 7.2).

On the matter of property rights, Victor Yannacone wrote:

> On July 9, 1969 the United States District Court for Colorado held
> that no federal court could interfere with the absolute right of private
> ownership, and the only way to save the fossil beds would be to buy
> them, at whatever price the speculators demanded. It was necessary
> to appeal to the Tenth Circuit Court of Appeals. The 34-million-year-
> old fossils were rescued twice by a last minute court order.[9]

Those orders held the line powerfully until Congress and the president could
act on the Florissant bill. Such rulings show how important a court's understanding of environmental values can be.

Figure 7.2. Landscape of the Florissant valley in winter. (Photograph by Lindsay Walker; courtesy of Florissant Fossil Beds National Monument.)

Richard Lamm pointed out in a 2008 interview that until 1969, "the law was really all against us. Property rights are very important in America, but particularly in the West. There was this idea that all land use [regulatory] devices were socialistic, if not worse, and that a person should have the right to do what they wanted with their own land." But he added, "We also recognized that the laws were changing. It was really very apparent by this time that there was going to be a whole new rethinking of the human role in the environment. This [case] was a risk worth taking."[10]

Despite the groundbreaking impact of the fossil beds case, lawyer and Defenders of Florissant chairman Roger Hansen still views private property rights as a bedrock of American law. In 2008, he stated:

A major stumbling block in the case was confronting what we knew would be a very conservative judicial and political philosophy which, unfortunately, has not progressed very much from where it was. Private property was, and continues to be, a peculiar American idol—much more so than in Europe. Private property "rights" are considered sacrosanct and many conservatives in Congress consider environmental regulation of any type as an unconstitutional "taking" of private property. We were not at all surprised to lose at the District Court level and would not have been surprised to lose at the Circuit Court of Appeals level, given the entrenched philosophy we were facing. If the "taking" issue had been firmly argued by the defendants, we might well not have prevailed.[11]

The Media—Information and Persuasion

As it turned out, the print and broadcast media played a significant role in keeping the public and government officials right up to date with developments on the Florissant issues. Colorado daily papers considered the battle for Florissant newsworthy. Editorial cartoonists from Denver papers helped create a humorous profile favorable to the case for preservation. In addition, *Science*, the *New York Times*, *National Geographic*, *Sports Illustrated*, and even the *New Yorker* helped spread the word nationally about the Florissant fossil beds lawsuit. *Time* retold the story after the fight was won.[12]

Vim Crane Wright, along with conservationists from the Colorado Mineral Society, organized her women friends and their children and invited the press to view a planned act of civil disobedience involving the blocking of bulldozers at Florissant on the critical day, July 29, 1969. Though the civil disobedience was ultimately unnecessary, publicity about the action captured imaginations far and wide. Vim was persuasive when interviewed on the radio. She also was strategic in using various media for fund raising, recruiting financial contributions from up and down the Rocky Mountains. The local PBS channel ran a special program in May 1969, laying out the issues related to the Florissant Fossil Beds National Monument proposal. Local newscasts also covered the issue at times.

Publicity brought in other volunteers, like Vim, who came out of the woodwork to help the Defenders of Florissant raise $12,000 or more during 1969. Without that generous support, the legal effort might not have been possible. As it was, the lawyers did not get paid. The funds raised covered the court costs and attorneys' travel expenses.

Science and Scientists

For more than one hundred years, scientists, in field and laboratory, built a path of scientific observations about fossil plants and animals, step by step, forward to the present. The observations have identified species, pointed to their nearest relatives today, and sketched out the climate and topography that must have existed in Colorado millions of years ago. The science of paleontology moved forward by leaps and bounds from the work of the early scientists who visited Florissant before 1900. Their work brought attention to hundreds of species of fossil plants and insects, the remnants of the biota that lived in and around the lake 34 million years ago.

The list of scientists who studied Florissant in the past was a "Who's Who" of well-recognized paleontologists—Samuel Scudder, Leo Lesquereux, T. D. A. Cockerell, and Harry MacGinitie. Contemporary scientists continue to make contributions to the scientific record. Paleobotanist Herb Meyer has published an exhaustively documented, lavishly illustrated book, *The Fossils of Florissant*, displaying and interpreting the main fossil types of Florissant.[13] Meyer, with Dena Smith of the University of Colorado, edited a Geological Society of America compendium of recent works on Florissant entitled *Paleontology of the Upper Eocene Florissant Formation, Colorado*.[14] In a 2003 volume printed by the Denver Museum of Nature & Science, *Fossil Flora and Stratigraphy of the Florissant Formation, Colorado*, Estella Leopold and Douglas Nichols of the U.S. Geological Survey have each added their stories based on the fossil pollen pulled out of the rocks.[15] In the same book, Elisabeth Wheeler[16] described the fossil woods, and Emmett Evanoff and his coauthors defined the different units that make up the Florissant Formation and determined the precise age of these rocks. These documentaries, and many more, now add to the academic literature on Florissant. Information is always being added as new studies about Florissant are undertaken. And, as Victor Yannacone said about research, it is also the way you build a court case, one brick at a time.

Conservationists

Ultimately, the conservation groups and the citizens were the real forces that influenced the media and Congress. Special note should be made of some of the local ranch owners who, out of love of the land, were premier conservationists and who helped to arouse interest in preserving the fossil beds and the land. Like Charlotte Hill, they also collected beautiful fossils. The collectors, especially the Singer family, were the first to build the case for government ownership and management of the fossil beds.

The stature of the individuals who comprised the Defenders of Florissant, Inc., was impressive; they represented diverse aspects of the academic, government, legal, and business communities. The leadership team of Bettie Willard, Estella Leopold, and Roger Hansen got the messages out to the public almost daily, printed bumper stickers, and were in weekly contact with members of Congress in the summer of 1969. The short-term importance of the Florissant campaign as an early environmental effort is that it won the attention of the public and the legislators. The long-term benefit was that the campaign succeeded and demonstrated that the American legal system can work. Building upon the Florissant victory, Colorado citizens and environmental groups felt their strength, and through the 1970s drove several more major environmental initiatives. These people, too, out of respect for the land, worked to protect various beautiful parts of Colorado. Each of the following Colorado campaigns utilized organizing, media, and legal strategies pioneered in the Florissant fossil beds campaign:

- Opposition to the uneconomical and environmentally destructive development of oil shale on public lands in western Colorado.

- Colorado participation in a national campaign that persuaded the U.S. Fish and Wildlife Service to halt the poisoning by ranchers of eagles and other raptors.

- Involvement in another national effort, spearheaded in Colorado by Vim Wright, to ban the use of poisonous cyanide guns to kill coyotes on public land.

- The successful bid, also led by Vim Wright, to establish a Colorado tax on hunting and fishing licenses that funded a nongame species management program.

- A voter-approved statewide referendum, organized by Richard Lamm, that rejected on environmental grounds a plan for the 1976 winter Olympics in Colorado.

- A legislative campaign, also headed by Richard Lamm, promoting passage of the first-ever state land use legislation.

- The congressional designation, with support from individuals and organizations nationwide, of several large Colorado wilderness areas, including the Gore-Eagles Nest (132,906 acres), Weminuche (433,745 acres), and Maroon Bells-Snowmass (181,117 acres).

- The defeat of the massive Two Forks dam project on the South Platte River near Denver.

- The vigorous opposition to Project Rulison, in which underground detonations of nuclear weapons were supposed to loosen natural gas from rock strata. (Though the detonations did occur, the litigation, spearheaded by Richard Lamm and Victor Yannacone, prevented large-scale flaring of the radioactive gases from the well; moreover, the political fallout was so substantial that no such nuclear gas fracturing projects have been attempted since that time.)

The fossil beds themselves were and are a treasure trove of inestimable value. As Congressman Roy Taylor of North Carolina said in support of the project, "We must understand that this area has scientific values not duplicated anywhere else in the world." These treasures, such as the huge petrified stumps (plate 6), need ongoing protection and interpretation. After the Defenders of Florissant disbanded, a new citizens' group with a different mission took up the Florissant banner. Volunteers from the Friends of the Florissant Fossil Beds watch out for the numerous needs of the monument. At the same time, the stalwart National Park Service staff has carried the torch for the burden of protecting the fossil beds and educating the visiting public since 1970. The rock gate sign at the entrance of the monument seems symbolic of the effort by the public to prevail over economic interests and to protect the fossil bed (figure 7.3).

New challenges to the research and interpretation of Florissant's fossils have arisen as federal law implemented in 2009 mandates restrictions on the kind of information that can be revealed to the public about fossil sites. Intended as a law to prevent illegal theft of fossils by unscrupulous collectors, these regulations impose restrictions, as an exemption to the Freedom of

Figure 7.3. The sign at the entrance to Florissant Fossil Beds National Monument is symbolic because it stands for the victory that popular support achieved over economic interests. (Photograph by Lindsay Walker; courtesy of Florissant Fossil Beds National Monument.)

Information Act, on revealing the specific locations of fossil sites. Not only does this "confidentiality" interfere with the integrity of the scientific process, it also stands as a potential obstacle to what visitors to federal fossil sites such as Florissant can be shown. After all of the efforts to protect Florissant so that science and education could continue, one has to wonder where the balances between protection, science, and education really lie.

Two principles are at stake as we face the future of our natural environments: one is the importance of the love of nature, and the other is the need for an environmental ethic. Perhaps the first to articulate the need for such an ethic was Aldo Leopold, who wrote in his book *A Sand County Almanac*:

> In short the land ethic changes the boundaries of the community to include soils, waters, plants and animals, or collectively the land. . . . Conservation is getting nowhere because it is incompatible with our Abrahamic concept of land. We abuse land because we regard it as a commodity belonging to us. When we see the land as a community to which we belong, we may begin to use it with love and respect. There is no other way for land to survive the impact of mechanized man, nor for us to reap from it the aesthetic harvest it is capable, under science, of contributing to culture.[17]

Richard Louv, in his book *Last Child in the Woods*, speaks to the love of nature.[18] We will need young people of the coming generations to stand up for the conservation and environmental values of our world. Preserving important resources, such as the Florissant Fossil Beds National Monument, will continue to provide a place for young and old alike to involve themselves with the wonders of our past and present.

Appendix

An Epoch Sealed in Stone:
A Guide to Florissant's Ancient Life and Fossils

ॐ

HERBERT W. MEYER

THE TOWERING LANDMARK OF PIKES PEAK DOMINATES THE GEOGRAphy of central Colorado. Just west of the 14,110-foot peak, and far below it, sits a very different kind of landmark—the grassy valley of Florissant in Teller County. If you visit the valley, you will see tan-colored layers of fossil-bearing volcanic ash exposed around the valley bottom and alongside roads. Volcanic ash consists of fine-grained rock, glass, and crystals ejected during explosive volcanic eruptions. A heavy ashfall across the landscape can lead to the immediate destruction of most of the local ecosystem. The weathered rocks at Florissant were once sediments and are remnants of an ancient lake that filled the basin now covered by the open meadows and grasslands of the modern Florissant valley (see plate 1). If you look north, cone-shaped Crystal Peak rises above the horizon. Pikes Peak, Crystal Peak, and huge, rounded rock outcrops surrounding the valley, like billion-year-old sentinels, are all formed of grayish-salmon-colored Pikes Peak Granite.

Except for the disappearance of the lake, the valley's physical landscape has changed remarkably little for millions of years. The plant and animal life inhabiting the Florissant valley is a different story, though, and the forest ecosystem of today is radically different from that of the distant past. Yet, the valley's former inhabitants are still on view—in the form of fossils.

Ancient Secrets Hidden in Plain Sight

The story of Florissant's famous fossils begins 34 million years ago in a dense forest along an ancient stream valley in the Rocky Mountains (plate 7A). Leaves freshly fallen from trees were carried gently in autumn winds, while insects buzzed with life in the forest. From time to time, ash and other debris from nearby volcanoes inundated the basin, burying plants, insects, and other animals beneath the waters of the lake. Through a unique set of circumstances, these organisms became inscribed in the annals of time, preserving an ancient world in stone.

The fossil beds entomb the remnants of an ancient ecosystem and encompass a great diversity of organisms ranging from tiny one-celled creatures to enormous trees and even mammals. But, scientific investigations at Florissant have uncovered much more than the identities of individual species. We now know a great deal about the life and times of this fleeting Florissant interval 34 to 35 million years ago. This was at the very end of the Eocene epoch. The Eocene was a prolonged warm period that lasted about 20 million years and was typified in the Rocky Mountains by warm temperate to subtropical climates. It was a period of great biotic diversity during which trees grew near the poles and the whole Earth was warm. When the worldwide climate cooled rather suddenly soon after Lake Florissant's existence, the region's flora scattered and a few species became extinct. The sharp cooling introduced a period called "Ice House Earth" in the early Oligocene about 32 to 33 million years ago, which eventually led to the Ice Ages beginning about 2.5 million years ago.

Before the major changes of Ice House Earth, Florissant was the last outpost in the Rocky Mountain region for a few subtropical plant species. In the long history of Earth, the Florissant ecosystem was one of a kind. In the modern world, there is no place else like it.

Fossilization in the Shadow of a Volcano

A flare-up of volcanic activity began in central Colorado 36.7 million years ago and lasted for several million years.[1] One of the first eruptions came as a cataclysmic fiery cloud erupted from a caldera fifty miles west of Florissant, leaving behind a sheet of rock in the Florissant valley known as the Wall Mountain Tuff. About 1 to 2 million years later, another volcano, known as the Guffey Volcano, became active about fifteen to twenty miles west of

Florissant, and it was this volcano's eruptions that initiated the preservation of Florissant's fossils. Now extinct and almost unrecognizable in the modern landscape, this high volcano dominated the skyline during the late Eocene epoch when Florissant's fossils were formed. Our understanding of the shape of the ancient landscape comes from the detailed mapping geologists have done over more than a century.

In a series of eruptions similar in style to the eruption of Washington's Mount St. Helens in 1980, volcanic ash fell across the landscape and wet volcanic mudflows sped down the flanks of the volcano eastward into the Florissant valley (plate 7B). Such flows are powerful, carrying trees and rocks and scouring the valley bottoms in their paths. The flows from the Guffey Volcano blocked a south-flowing stream, thereby forming Lake Florissant (plate 8). The geologic map (plate 9) and cross section (plate 10) show the extent of the ancient lake and its relation to the volcano. Periodic volcanic ashfalls and sediment flows accumulated along the valley's bottom, its upper slopes, and in the new lake, where the layered sediments are now known as the Florissant Formation (figure A.1).[2] These are the rocks that hold the secrets of Florissant's past.

One of the mudflows from the Guffey Volcano churned along the Florissant stream valley prior to the formation of the lake, piling up around trees and burying the forest in a layer of volcanic sediments about 15 feet (5 meters) thick. These sediments hardened into a rock that

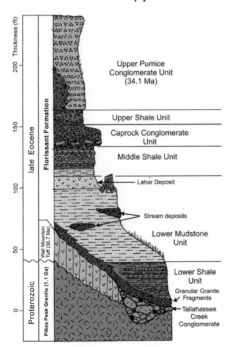

Figure A.1. The different rock formations in the Florissant area are illustrated in this stratigraphic column and include the Pikes Peak Granite, Wall Mountain Tuff, and Florissant Formation. The Florissant Formation is divided into six units. Ga = billion years; Ma = million years. The tree stump symbol indicates the position of the petrified stumps in the volcanic mudflow. (Courtesy of Emmett Evanoff.)

encased the bases of the large trees, preserving them as stumps. Groundwater passing through the rock extracted the mineral silica. As water-borne silica permeated the porous wood of the trees, the silica hardened again within the cells of the wood, petrifying the trees. Some of the original cellular matter of the trees still remains, and when microscopic thin sections are examined, details of wood anatomy are clearly evident. The trees, largely *Sequoia* (redwood) and remarkably well preserved, were probably abundant in the valley and scraps of fossil wood are common. Foliage and cones of *Sequoia* are also abundant in the lake shale.

After one of the volcanic mudflows blocked the stream drainage, Lake Florissant began to fill. Volcanic ash coming from the Guffey Volcano or other volcanic sources in the region was deposited into the lake and settled to the bottom along with the frustules, or "shells," of tiny diatoms—microscopic algae that lived in the lake waters. Together, the volcanic ash and diatoms formed layered sediments on the bottom of the lake. These sediments entombed the remains of leaves and insects that had fallen there. These remains were gradually flattened and compressed to form fossils as the sediment began compacting to become shale.

Figure A.2. The lower shale unit of the Florissant Formation is exposed at the Florissant Fossil Quarry, which is a private site owned by the Clare family outside the boundaries of the monument. Denver Museum of Nature & Science paleobotanist Ian Miller is on the left and National Park Service paleontologist Herb Meyer is on the right. (Courtesy of Steve Wagner.)

Figure A.3. Delicate layers of the thin paper shale can be split to expose fossil leaves and insects. (Photograph by Lindsay Walker; courtesy of Florissant Fossil Beds National Monument.)

The lake shale is exposed today as rock outcrops around the Florissant valley. There are three different shale units in the Florissant Formation (see figure A.1), each formed by thick accumulations of sediment (figure A.2). As the shale weathers, it can be split apart into thin layers—less than a millimeter in thickness—known as "paper shale." Peeling these delicate layers apart opens the pages of an ancient book, revealing for the first time the fine print of its contents—the detailed impressions of leaves and insects that tell the story of a bygone ecosystem (figure A.3).

The Fossil Organisms of Florissant

The most conspicuous fossils that Florissant visitors see are the huge petrified stumps of the extinct redwood, *Sequoia affinis.* Most of the thirty or so fossil stumps known to exist still stand upright in their original growth positions. Reports suggest that there were many more logs and stumps before late-nineteenth- and early twentieth-century tourists carted them away.[3] Several of the stumps were excavated by early developers of the site, who completely exposed them to the elements so that they could be viewed as tourist attractions. In one case, dynamite apparently was used to remove the surrounding rock.[4]

The largest petrified stump at Florissant measures 13.5 feet (4.1 meters) in diameter at breast height, whereas the Big Stump measures 12.1 feet (3.7 meters). Perhaps the most unusual stump of the group is the Redwood Trio (see plate 6), made up of three interconnected trunks that are part of one individual. This genetic clone arose from vegetative sprouting around the base of an original parent trunk that decayed as the trio of trunks grew to maturity. The habit of stump sprouting, which the trio probably represents, is characteristic of today's coastal redwood, *Sequoia sempervirens*. Besides the redwoods, at least five other kinds of hardwood trees at Florissant have been identified from their petrified woods.[5]

The Florissant flora includes a wealth of species. In addition to those known from fossil wood, at least 130 different types of trees that grew in the ancient forest are identified from impressions of leaves, fruits, seeds, and pollen preserved in the lake shale (plate 11).[6] Many of these are similar to plants that we know today. Others, representing extinct species or genera (groups of related species), are very different from modern plants. The two most common plant fossils at Florissant, the beech-like *Fagopsis* and elm-like *Cedrelospermum*, are actually extinct genera. *Asterocarpinus* and *Florissantia*, both known from their fruits, are also extinct. Some of the fossil impressions show attached leaves, flowers, and fruits, making it possible to reconstruct the characteristics of extinct genera from different organs of the same plant. Other plants, similar to their modern relatives, are easily recognized by anyone familiar with common trees and shrubs today. These include pines, oaks, hickories, poplars, mulberries, hawthorns, roses, plums, redbuds, bladdernuts, golden-rain trees, maples, and sumacs.

More evidence about ancient plant life comes from fossil pollen and spores, which were dispersed by wind or insects during the process of pollination.[7] These microfossils were preserved in the lake shale as wind-borne pollen landed on the surface of the lake and sank, mixing with the volcanic ash and diatom sediments on the bottom. In the laboratory, shale can be dissolved in various acids, leaving behind the sturdy and resistant pollen grains, which then can be mounted on microscopic slides for study. Pollen grains from different kinds of plants have many different shapes and sizes. Sculpturing on the pollen surface and construction of the pollen wall are often very ornate. About 150 different types of pollen and spores can be recognized at Florissant, including some from plants that are not found in the fossil record of leaves and fruits. Some of the pollen, such as spruce and fir, probably came from plants that were more distant from the lake, providing a more complete picture of the composition of the surrounding forest.

Seemingly unlikely candidates for fossilization, insects and spiders are among the most delicate fossils (plate 12). The fine veins of wings and tiny "hairs" are visible in some of the shales. Some show the minute details of compound eyes, as if still gazing at the world after 34 million years. Yet together, insects and spiders are by far the most diverse group of fossil organisms at Florissant. So far, paleontologists have described a total of some seventeen hundred species from Florissant, of which more than fifteen hundred are insects and spiders.[8]

Most of the major orders of insects are represented at Florissant, including mayflies, dragonflies, grasshoppers and crickets, mantids, flies, cockroaches, termites, earwigs, web spinners, bugs, lacewings and snakeflies, beetles, scorpionflies, caddisflies, butterflies and moths, and ants, bees, and wasps. Among these groups, the beetles dominate in number of species, just as they do in the modern world. More surprisingly, species of butterflies are diverse, despite how unlikely their fossilization may seem, and even caterpillars have been found. Winged ants, which represent the ones that reproduce in ant communities, are also common. Mayflies, whose adult life stage may have lasted but a day or two after they emerged from the water to mate, provide the briefest glimpse of an instant in time from Colorado's past. A variety of spider fossils have been found, some with long outstretched legs radiating from their bodies, imprinting in stone the appearance of a stalking spider waiting in its web.

Fossilized vertebrates are much less common at Florissant (plate 13), but they nonetheless provide important clues about the overall ecology of this ancient community. Fish include bowfins (some more than 16 inches [40 centimeters] in length), pirate perches, suckers, and catfish. All except the pirate perch were bottom dwellers. Several birds have been found, including a roller, a cuckoo, and a complete shore bird.

The fossil remains of mammals at Florissant are few and fragmentary. Most of them, such as the giant rhinoceros-like brontothere or sheep-like oreodont, are extinct and unlike any that we know today. A small mouse opossum was found in the lake shale (see plate 13A), but most of the mammal fossils have come from floodplain deposits that formed along the ancient stream valley. Work since 2003 has tripled the number of mammals known from Florissant, made up primarily of small forms such as rodents, lagomorphs (rabbits and hares), and North America's oldest known mole.[9] Such discoveries show that exciting new knowledge still remains to be uncovered, even though fossils have been collected and researched at Florissant for more than 130 years. Without a national monument to protect these fossils and help to promote their study, they might have been lost forever.

CONCENTRATIONS OF FLORISSANT GENERA TODAY

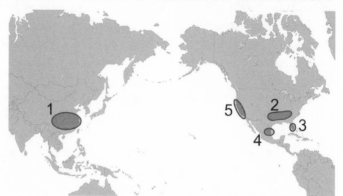

Figure A.4. Map showing areas where modern genera similar to those in the fossil record at Florissant are restricted today. Many living relatives of Florissant plant genera are widespread in temperate to subtropical mixed conifer and hardwood forests. Clusters of such genera occur today in several notable areas: (1) central and southern China, (2) Ozark Plateau to southern Appalachians, (3) southern Florida, (4) central and northeastern Mexico, and (5) western California. (Map drafted by Kate Sweeny and Stephanie Zaborac-Reed; courtesy of the University of Washington.)

Even with such high biological diversity, not all of the organisms that probably lived in the area are represented in the fossil record. Many factors determine what is, and is not, fossilized. For example, the leaves of deciduous trees that grew near the lake had a much greater chance of becoming fossilized simply because they were shed in greater numbers and fell directly into the lake. The leaves of evergreen trees growing on more distant ridges were shed less frequently and in fewer numbers, and were never transported far enough to reach the water. Likewise, winged insects that could fly over the lake were more likely to end up in the water, and insects with durable exoskeletons, such as beetles, had a better chance of fossilization than those with softer bodies.

It is a mystery as to why no reptiles or amphibians have ever been described from Florissant. Apparently, whatever frogs, salamanders, and turtles may have lived here never became fossilized. What we find in the fossil record are only parts of the ancient ecosystem. Although some pieces of this puzzle may be missing, the huge number of organisms in the fossil record at Florissant allows us to reconstruct much of the forest ecosystem that once predominated in this region of present-day Colorado.

Stories from an Extinct Ecosystem

Florissant is a name that brings immediate recognition and awe to the minds of paleontologists the world over. It is here that a strikingly rich volume in the library of Earth's history and its life is preserved, with pages beautifully intact for all to read and understand.

Each individual fossil tells the story of a once-living organism. By studying the fossils of a particular group of organisms and comparing them to fossils from other places and to similar modern organisms, patterns of change become evident. Geographic dispersal, extinction, and evolution through time can be traced. The stories of all of these individual organisms at Florissant, together with what is known about how ecosystems work, allow us to form a strikingly detailed picture of an ancient, extinct ecosystem of the Eocene epoch, unlike any place in the modern world. By themselves, fossils may be very small, but taken together they offer tremendous insight into the past.

One of the most striking things that visitors recognize on coming to Florissant is the contrast between the plants and animals found in the fossil record and those that live in the modern forest. There is much less diversity in the cool temperate mountain valley today in comparison to life during the warmth of the late Eocene 34 million years ago. Today's coniferous forest of pine, spruce, and Douglas fir, interspersed with groves of aspen, contrasts sharply with what we see in the fossil record. While the fossils reveal a warm temperate forest that included some pines and spruces, they also show that there were many broad-leaved hardwoods such as hickory, redbud, tree of heaven, West Indies cedar, golden-rain tree, and many others that no longer live in the Florissant region. Even palms once grew here. Some of these plants now live only in places as far away as China or Mexico (figure A.4). Among the fossil insects at Florissant, tsetse flies now live only in tropical Africa, and among the birds, cuckoos and rollers are now restricted to the Eastern Hemisphere. Most of the Florissant mammals are unrecognized today.

Plants are relatively accurate indicators of climate, which is evident when driving from the lowlands into the mountains or traveling from the tropics to the arctic. Changes in vegetation result from progressively cooler temperatures as one travels higher in elevation or latitude. Studies of modern vegetation and its relation to climate provide the basis for interpreting past climates and climate change. Comparison of fossils to modern plants shows that the late Eocene climate at Florissant was much warmer than today with mild winters. Over time, the climate changed, eventually becoming the cool temperate and drier climate of today. Much of this change is explained by global cooling that took place in the million years or so following the deposition of the Florissant fossils. The mix of temperate and subtropical plants and insects led some paleontologists, such as Harry MacGinitie, to suppose that the elevation during the Eocene might have been lower than the present, at only 3,000 feet (900 meters), but other scientists think that Florissant was already near its present elevation of about 8,200 feet (2,500 meters) or even higher 34 million years ago.[10] Certainly, global climate change was a key cause of the differences we see between the ancient and modern forests, and Florissant helps us to understand how this process affects life on the planet.

The forest community around Lake Florissant probably represented a mosaic of habitats.[11] Near the stream or lake, where moisture was plentiful, tall redwood trees and white cedars would have flourished along with an understory of *Fagopsis*, *Cedrelospermum*, poplars, hickories, and maples. Conditions were drier along the ridges above the lake, and here grew oaks, mountain mahogany, and pines in more open woodlands. Even higher, perhaps along the slopes of the Guffey Volcano, there was a conifer forest of pines, firs, and spruces. Insects, too, would have varied among these environments, with caddisflies, dragonflies, and crane flies being tied to the moist forest closer to the lake. The nature of a forest also helps to determine what kinds of larger animals can live in an area, because plants provide the food source for herbivorous mammals.

Some aspects of the ancient ecosystem can be observed at a much smaller scale than that of the whole forest. For example, many of the fossil leaves show holes and other feeding patterns (see *Paracarpinus* in plate 11) that demonstrate the interaction between plants and insects as a response to climatic changes through time.[12] These features help us to understand how plants and insects have co-evolved, and how plants may have responded in their evolution to increased feeding by insects. Other leaf fossils show galls or leaf mines, formed as an insect's larva developed within the plant tissues. Within remarkable fossils such as these, it is possible to see traces of several phases during a single insect's life cycle.

With so much information available to us, it is easy to let our imaginations run freely with that knowledge in recreating this ancient world of 34 million years ago. Imagine the chirping of crickets or the singing of katydids as they rubbed their legs together, the humming of the dragonfly's wings, the rustling of the branches of the high redwoods in the wind, or the snapping branches of brush as the giant brontothere browsed. They are but images in stone today, but these fossils are the representative portraits of an extraordinary diversity of characters in a Florissant ecosystem that was once alive and flourishing.

Many of the organisms found at Florissant are unique or very rare in the fossil record and belong to species now considered extinct. For example, with twelve species in eleven genera, Florissant has a greater known diversity of fossil butterflies than any other site in the world.[13] Like so many other Florissant fossils, these insects show remarkable preservation. In some cases even the patterns that corresponded with coloration on the butterflies' wings are preserved (see figure 1.2).

Florissant fossils continue to provide new information about the processes of evolution, both of particular groups of organisms and entire biotic communities. Not only are evolutionary patterns of interactions between plants and herbivorous insects evident, but new studies of fossil diatoms from Florissant are contributing to our understanding of the early diversification of these organisms in freshwater environments.[14] Fossils showing leaves attached to fruits have shed new light on evolutionary patterns within plant families such as the birches, beeches, and elms.[15]

Combined with evidence from other fossil sites, Florissant holds important evidence about how an entire ecosystem evolved in response to global climate change. The community became extinct as a consequence of the change. Looking back at Florissant's past gives us the foresight to better understand the possible consequences of global climate change in the world today.

Florissant's striking natural setting and wide array of plant and animal fossils give it an aura of magic. The valley, now largely a part of Florissant Fossil Beds National Monument, provides an opportunity to study a time extraordinarily unlike that of the present. The area has tremendous recreational and aesthetic values, as well. The chance to hike among the fossilized remains of redwood giants or to witness the discovery of a tiny 34-million-year-old flower or insect makes for an experience both rare and memorable.

Notes

❦

INTRODUCTION

1. Victor John Yannacone, jr., Bernard S. Cohen, and Steven G. Davison, *Environmental Rights and Remedies*, vol. 1 (New York: Lawyers Co-operative Pub. Co., 1972), 1–317.
2. Estella B. Leopold and Scott T. Clay-Poole, "Fossil Leaf and Pollen Floras of Colorado Compared: Climatic Implications," in *Fossil Flora and Stratigraphy of the Florissant Formation, Colorado. Proceedings of the Denver Museum of Nature & Science* 4, no. 1, ed. Emmett Evanoff, Kathryn M. Gregory-Wodzicki, and Kirk R. Johnson (Denver: Denver Museum of Nature & Science, 2001) 17–69.
3. S. H. Scudder, "Tertiary Lake-Basin at Florissant, Colorado, between South and Hayden Parks," *Bulletin of United States Geological & Geographical Survey of the Territories* 6, no. 2 (1881): 281.
4. Scudder, "Tertiary Lake-Basin at Florissant," 288.
5. U.S. Senate, Committee on Interior and Insular Affairs, Subcommittee on Parks and Recreation, *A Bill to Provide for the Establishment of the Florissant Fossil Beds National Monument in the State of Colorado: Hearing on S. 912,* 91st Cong., 1st sess. (May 29, 1969), 33.

CHAPTER ONE

1. Steven W. Veatch and Herbert W. Meyer, "History of Paleontology at the Florissant Fossil Beds, Colorado," in *Paleontology of the Upper Eocene Florissant Formation, Colorado: Geological Society of America Special Paper 435,* ed. Herbert W. Meyer and Dena M. Smith (Boulder, CO: Geological Society of America, 2008), 1–18; James McChristal, "A History of Florissant Fossil Beds National Monument: In Celebration of Preservation," unpublished report, 1994, FLFO-423, Florissant Fossil Beds National Monument Archives, Colorado.
2. A. C. Peale, "Report of A. C. Peale M.D., Geologist of the South Park Division," *Annual Report of the United States Geological and Geographical Survey of the Territories* 7 (1874): 193–273, 20 plates.

3. Leo Lesquereux, "Lignitic Formation and Fossil Flora," *United States Geological Survey of the Territories Annual Report* 6 (1873): 317–427.

4. Leo Lesquereux, "Contribution to the Fossil Flora of the Western Territories, pt. II: The Tertiary Flora," *United States Geological Survey of the Territories Report* 7 (1878): 1–366, 65 plates; Leo Lesquereux, "Contribution to the Fossil Flora of the Western Territories, pt. III: The Cretaceous and Tertiary Floras," *United States Geological Survey of the Territories Report* 8 (1883): 1–283, 60 plates.

5. Edward Drinker Cope published several papers on the Florissant fossil fish, including "On the Fishes of the Tertiary Shales of the South Park," *United States Geological and Geographical Survey of the Territories* 2, no. 1 (1875): 3–5.

6. Michael F. Kohl, John S. McIntosh, and John H. Ostrom, *Discovering Dinosaurs in the Old West: The Field Journals of Arthur Lakes* (Washington, D.C.: Smithsonian Institution Press, 1997).

7. Arthur Lakes, "Map of Sedimentary Lacustrine Basin at Florissant near South Park," February 20, 1878, FLFO-1013, Florissant Fossil Bed National Monument Archives, Colorado. Reprinted in Herbert Meyer, *The Fossils of Florissant* (Washington, D.C.: Smithsonian Books, 2003), 9, fig. 8.

8. Frank M. Carpenter, "A Review of Our Present Knowledge of the Geological History of the Insects," *Psyche* 37 (1930): 15–34, 1 plate.

9. Samuel H. Scudder, "The Tertiary Insects of North America," *United States Geological Survey of the Territories Report* 13, (1890): 1–734, 28 plates.

10. T. D. A. Cockerell, "Colorado a Million Years Ago," *American Museum Journal* 16, no. 7 (1916): 442–50.

11. Liz Brosius, "The Collector," *Earth* 4, no. 1 (1995): 50–57.

12. Frank M. Carpenter, "Superclass Hexapoda," in *Treatise on Invertebrate Paleontology, Part R, Arthropoda 4*, ed. R. L. Kaesler, vol. 3 and 4 (Boulder, CO: Geological Society of America; Lawrence: University of Kansas, 1992), 655, plates 1–75.

13. Harry D. MacGinitie, *Fossil Plants of the Florissant Beds, Colorado*, Carnegie Institution of Washington publication 599 (Washington, D.C.: Carnegie Institution of Washington, 1953), 1–198, plates 1–75.

14. *Fairplay Flume*, June 17, 1880, 1.

15. "Petrified Stumps," *Colorado Springs Gazette*, April 8, 1876.

16. Summary statement of property assets for the sale of Coplen Petrified Forest, by J. D. Coplen, November 1924, FLFO-1270:3–6, Florissant Fossil Beds National Monument Archives, Colorado.

17. Toby Wells, telephone conversation with Herb Meyer, August 2011.

18. Agnes Singer, interview by Henry Tanski, February 25, 1976, tape 108T transcript, FLFO-166, Florissant Fossil Beds National Monument Archives, Colorado.

19. Toby Wells, telephone conversation.

20. "In a Forest of Stone: A Wonderful Show of Petrified Wood in a Colorado Valley," *The Mineralogist's Monthly* 6, no. 10 (August 1891): 118–19.

21. *Denver Post*, August 14, 1911.

22. Ibid.

23. *Denver Times*, October 12, 1915.

24. Edmund B. Rogers and Edwin C. Alberts, *Florissant Fossil Shale Beds, Colorado*, report prepared for the National Park Service, January 1953. This source also mentions the 1932 report by Roger Toll.

25. National Park Service Acting Regional Director I. J. Castro to Agnes R. Singer, February 1958, FLFO-1270:61, Florissant Fossil Beds National Monument Archives, Colorado; National Park Service Chief of Division of Recreation Resource Planning Ben H. Thompson to Agnes R. Singer, August 16, 1961, FLFO-1270:62, Florissant Fossil Beds National Monument Archives, Colorado.

26. National Park Service, Midwest Region, *A Proposed Florissant Fossil Beds National Monument, Colorado*, April 1962.

CHAPTER TWO

1. National Park Service, Midwest Region, *A Proposed Florissant Fossil Beds National Monument, Colorado*, April 1962.

2. U.S. Senate, Committee on Interior and Insular Affairs, Subcommittee on Parks and Recreation, *A Bill to Provide for the Establishment of the Florissant Fossil Beds National Monument in the State of Colorado*, S. 912, 91st Cong., 1st sess., 50.

3. Aldo Leopold, *A Sand County Almanac* (New York: Oxford University Press, 1949).

4. Estella B. Leopold and Richard A. Scott, "Pollen and Spores and Their Use in Geology," in *Smithsonian Institution Annual Report for 1957*, publication 4322 (Washington, D.C.: Smithsonian Institution), 303–23.

5. Harry D. MacGinitie, *Fossil Plants of the Florissant Beds, Colorado*, Carnegie Institution of Washington publication 599 (Washington, D.C.: Carnegie Institution of Washington, 1953), 1–198, plates 1–75.

6. Estelle Brown, "Florissant Fossil Fight for Future," unpublished manuscript, 1969, FLFO-424, Florissant Fossil Beds National Monument Archives, Colorado.

7. Brown, "Florissant Fossil Fight for Future."

8. Estella B. Leopold, on behalf of the Conservation Committee and the Colorado Mountain Club, to Representative Wayne Aspinall, August 19, 1966, in the author's private collection.

9. Eleanor Gamer, "Under Consideration for National Monument Status Are: The Fossil Beds of Florissant," *National Parks Magazine* 39, no. 214 (1965).

10. Roger Hansen, "A Blueprint for Action: Now or Never," presentation, Colorado Open Space Coordinating Council, Breckinridge, CO, September 27, 1964. He also gave a summary talk in 1995 on the formation of COSCC, "A Colorado Conservation Agenda: 31 Years After Breckenridge," presented to the Colorado Environmental Coalition on the thirty-first anniversary of the Colorado Open Space Council.

11. Frank Evans to Roger Hansen, June 16, 1966, in author's private collection.

12. Colorado Open Space Coordinating Council, "Conservation Support," news release, June 15, 1966, FLFO-424, Florissant Fossil Beds National Monument Archives, Colorado.

13. Susan Marsh, "Preserving Colorado's Rich Fossil Fields," *New York Times*, July 17, 1966.

14. Henry Lansford, "Treasure in Stone," *Denver Post Empire Magazine*, December 4, 1966.

15. Estella Leopold, "Housing Subdivision vs. Florissant Fossils," *Trail & Timberline*, no. 573 (September 1966): 162.

16. Rocky Mountain National Park superintendent Granville Liles to National Park Service, Midwest Region, regional director, memorandum, "Subject: NPS Representative, Colorado—Visit to Proposed Florissant Fossil Beds NM [National Monument]," September 24, 1964, FLFO-166, FLFO-1270:59, Florissant Fossil Beds National Monument Archives, Colorado.

17. MacGinitie, *Fossil Plants of the Florissant Beds, Colorado.*

18. Nate Snare, conversation with Estella Leopold, 1964.

19. Advisory Board on National Parks, Historic Sites, Buildings and Monuments, memorandum, October 7, 1965, FLFO-424, Florissant Fossil Beds National Monument Archives, Colorado.

20. National Park Service, *Master Plan for Proposed Florissant Fossil Beds National Park*, May 1967.

21. *Florissant Fossil Beds National Monument*, H.R. 5065, 90th Cong., Cong. Rec., (February 16, 1967): H1487.

22. Assistant Secretary of the Interior Clarence F. Pautzke to Senator Wayne Aspinall, September 5, 1967, FLFO-424, Florissant Fossil Beds National Monument Archives, Colorado.

23. Colorado Open Space Coordinating Council, "Statement in Support of Florissant Fossil Beds National Monument," news release, March 15, 1968, 1–3 with map, FLFO-424, Florissant Fossil Beds National Monument Archives, Colorado.

24. Bettie Willard and Oakleigh Thorne II to Stanley Cain, letter containing University of Colorado's Natural Areas Committee's "Evaluation of the Scientific and Educational Values of Florissant Fossil Beds," February 5, 1968, FLFO-424, Florissant Fossil Beds National Monument Archives, Colorado.

25. Assistant Secretary of Interior Stanley Cain to National Park Service director, memorandum, "Subject: Florissant Interest of Sen. Allott," March 13, 1968, FLFO-424, Florissant Fossil Beds National Monument Archives, Colorado.

26. Stanley Cain to National Park Service director.

27. *Introduction of Bill Relating to Florissant Fossil Beds National Monument, S. 912*, 91st Cong., 1st sess., Cong. Rec. (February 4, 1969): S1228.

28. University of Colorado Natural Areas Committee, "Evaluation of the Scientific and Educational Values of Florissant Fossil Beds," 1968, FLFO-424, Florissant Fossil Beds National Monument Archives, Colorado.

29. Wayne Aspinall to Betty Willard, March 10, 1969, FLFO-424, Florissant Fossil Beds National Monument Archives, Colorado.

30. *Introduction of Bill Relating to Florissant Fossil Beds National Monument, S. 912,* S1227.

31. Brown, "Florissant Fossil Fight for Future."

32. Berton Roueché, "A Reporter at Large: A Window on the Oligocene," *The New Yorker*, November 13, 1971, 141–55.

33. Colorado Open Space Coordinating Council, "Statement in Support of Establishing Florissant Fossil Beds National Monument, Teller Co., Colorado," March 1969, FLFO-424, Florissant Fossil Beds National Monument Archives, Colorado.

CHAPTER THREE

1. Jeffrey Olen, "Negotiating for Two Years: Real Estate Firm Denies Profit Motive in Florissant Land Deal," *Colorado Springs Free Press*, July 4, 1969.

2. Olen, "Negotiating for Two Years."

3. Ibid.

4. Luther J. Carter, "DDT Critics Attempt to Ban Its Use in Wisconsin," *Science* 163, no. 3867 (February 7, 1969): 548–50.

5. Luther J. Carter, "Conservation Law II: Scientists Play a Key Role in Court Suits," *Science* 166, no. 3913 (December 26, 1969): 1601–6.

6. Carter, "Conservation Law II."

7. Estella Leopold to National Park Service director George B. Hartzog, May 23, 1969; Beatrice Willard to George B. Hartzog, May 20, 1969; Department of Natural Resources to George B. Hartzog, May 19, 1969; Board of County Commissioners to George B Hartzog, May 20, 1969; Undersecretary of the Interior Russell E. Train to chair of the Senate Committee on Interior and Insular Affairs, Senator Henry M. Jackson, letter with "staffing plan" enclosure. All correspondence from Florissant Fossil Beds National Monument Archives, Colorado.

8. *A Bill to Provide for the Establishment of the Florissant Fossil Beds National Monument in the State of Colorado: Hearing on S. 912, Before the Comm. on Interior and Insular Affairs Subcomm. on Parks and Recreation*, 91st Cong., 1st Sess. (May 29, 1969), 1.

9. *A Bill to Provide for the Establishment of the Florissant Fossil Beds National Monument in the State of Colorado: Hearing on S. 912* (statement of Joe Burns), 27.

10. Ibid. (statement of Harry D. MacGinitie), 32–36.

11. Ibid. (statement of Harry D. MacGinitie), 32–36.

12. Ibid. (statement of Beatrice E. Willard), 38–41.

13. Ibid. (statement of Estella B. Leopold), 42–44.

14. Ibid. (statement of Richard Beidleman), 50–51.

15. Ibid. (statement of Peter Robinson), 56.

16. Ibid. (statement of John Chronic), 47–49.

17. Ibid. (statement of Richard C. Bradley), 60–64.

18. Philip M. Boffey, "Famous Fossil Beds Are Endangered," *Science* 164, no. 3884 (June 6, 1969): 1151.

19. "Acquisition of Fossil Bed Land May Be Speeded, Allott Says," *Denver Post*, August 23, 1969.

20. Board of County Commissioners, Teller County, Colorado, *Resolution*, Report No. 201993, June 19, 1969.

21. Victor John Yannacone, jr., Bernard S. Cohen, and Steven G. Davison, *Environmental Rights and Remedies*, vol. 1 (New York: Lawyers Co-operative Pub. Co., 1972): 56–57.

CHAPTER FOUR

1. *Defenders of Florissant, Inc. v. Park Land Co.*, C-1539 (D. Colo., July 9, 1969), verified complaint "Prayer for Relief."

2. *Defenders of Florissant, Inc. v. Park Land Co.*, C-1539 (D. Colo., July 9, 1969), verified complaint, 8(b).

3. Victor John Yannacone, jr., Bernard S. Cohen, and Steven G. Davison, *Environmental Rights and Remedies*, vol. 1 (New York: Lawyers Co-operative Pub. Co., 1972).

4. Yannacone et al., *Environmental Rights and Remedies*.

5. James C. Thompson, "The Florissant Affair: An Exposé" (term paper, Professor Henry Caulfield, Department of Recreation and Watershed Resources, Colorado State University, spring semester 1970), 1–28.

6. *Defenders of Florissant, Inc. v. Park Land Co.*, No. 340-69 (10th Cir. 1969), oral argument of Victor John Yannacone, jr.

7. Ibid.

8. *Defenders of Florissant, Inc. vs. Park Land Co.*, No. 340-69 (10th Cir. 1969), temporary restraining order.

9. Barbara Browne, "Court Halts Fossil Bed Project," *Rocky Mountain News*, July 11, 1969, with photo.

10. Dan Gibson, "The Tools for the Job," *Rocky Mountain News*, June 8, 1969.

11. Zygmunt J. B. Plater, Robert H. Abrams, William Goldfarb, Robert L. Graham, and Lisa Heinzerling, *Environmental Law and Policy: Nature, Law, and Society*, 3rd ed. (New York: Aspen, 2004).

12. William H. Rodgers Jr., "The Most Creative Moments in the History of Environmental Law: 'The What's,'" *University of Illinois Law Review* 2000, no. 1 (2000).

13. Victor John Yannacone, jr., written statement to Estella Leopold, e-mail, November 20, 2011.

14. Richard Lamm, telephone conversation with Estella Leopold, July 1969, notes in author's private collection and Florissant Fossil Beds National Monument Archives, Colorado.

CHAPTER FIVE

1. "Florissant Company Seeks to Kill Order," *Denver Post*, July 16, 1969.

2. Barbara Browne, "Fossil Beds Unit in Fiscal Trouble," *Rocky Mountain News*, August 2, 1969.

3. Vim Crane Wright, interview by Nancy Dahl, August 2000, in author's private collection; reprinted with permission from John A. C. Wright.

4. Richard Lamm, interview by John Stansfield, December 17, 2008, in author's private collection.

5. Victor Yannacone, jr., written statement to Estella Leopold, November 20, 2011, in author's private collection.

6. Yannacone, written statement.

7. Ibid.

8. Ibid.

9. Ibid.

10. Appellant's Brief, No. 403–69, at 12 (10th Cir. 1969), filed July 29, 1969.

11. Victor Yannacone, jr., written statement.

12. Earlier restraining order applies: "It is ordered that the temporary restraining order entered on July 10, 1969, is extended and continued in full force and effect until further order of this court. It is further ordered that the appeal from the order of the United States District Court for the District of Colorado denying a preliminary injunction will be heard on the merits in Denver, Colorado, at 9:30 am on Monday." Order filed July 29, 1969, No. 403–69 (10th Cir. 1969).

13. Victor Yannacone, jr., written statement.

14. Tom Lamm, phone interview by Estella Leopold, April 2010; "Tom Lamm," Florissant Fossil Beds National Monument 40th Anniversary DVD (unpublished material, FLFO-430, Florissant Fossil Beds National Monument Archives, Colorado), 2009.

15. Victor Yannacone, jr., written statement.

16. Nate Snare, telephone conversation with Estella Leopold, July 30, 1969.

17. Holly Buchan to Estella Leopold, e-mail, April 23, 2010; reprinted with permission.

18. "Colorado Delegation Urges Work Halt on Fossil Beds," *Rocky Mountain News*, August 7, 1969.

19. *Florissant Fossil Beds National Monument, Colo., S. 912*, 91st Cong., 1st Sess., Cong. Rec. (August 4, 1969): H6803.

20. *Florissant Fossil Beds National Monument, Colo., S. 912*, H6807.

21. "Tom Lamm," Florissant Fossil Beds National Monument 40th Anniversary DVD.

CHAPTER SIX

1. National Park Service Division of Land Acquisition map of Florissant Fossil Beds National Monument, compiled August 1969 from basic land ownership data of March 1967, FLFO-6306, Florissant Fossil Beds National Monument Archives, Colorado.

2. Toby Wells, telephone conversation with Herb Meyer, August 2011.

3. Elizabeth Craig, narrative of oral history interview by Mike McClain, October 9, 1996, FLFO-271, FLFO-3061, Florissant Fossil Beds National Monument Archives, Colorado.

4. Ranger Richard L. Shillinglaw, unpublished journal, August–November 1970, FLFO-202, Florissant Fossil Beds National Monument Archives, Colorado.

5. Secretary of the Interior Nathanial Reed to Senator H. Jackson, July 5, 1974, cited in James McChristal, "A History of Florissant Fossil Beds National Monument: In Celebration of Preservation," (unpublished report, Florissant Fossil Beds National Monument Archives, FLFO-423, 1994), 27.

6. House Committee on Interior and Insular Affairs, *Providing for the Establishment of the Florissant Fossil Beds National Monument in the State of Colorado*, H.R. Rep. No. 91–411, at 1 (July 31, 1969).

7. Jack Williams, interview by Shawn Frizzell, 2008, Florissant Fossil Beds National Monument Archives, Colorado.

8. Williams, interview.

9. *Fairplay Flume*, June 17, 1880, 1.

10. Harry D. MacGinitie, interview by Earle Kittleman, September 21, 1979, FLFO-375, Florissant Fossil Beds National Monument Archives, Colorado.

11. Undersecretary of the Interior Russell E. Train to Chair of the Senate Committee on Interior and Insular Affairs, Senator Henry M. Jackson, letter with "staffing plan" enclosure, Florissant Fossil Beds National Monument Archives, Colorado.

12. H.R. Rep. No. 91–411, at 1–6 (July 31, 1969).

13. H.R. Rep. No. 91–411, at 2 (July 31, 1969).

14. F. Martin Brown examined the Florissant fossil insect collections at several museums, and his extensive collection of notes, correspondence, and photographs is in the Florissant Fossil Beds National Monument Archives, Colorado.

15. Harry D. MacGinitie, *Fossil Plants of the Florissant Beds, Colorado*, Carnegie Institution of Washington publication 599 (Washington, D.C.: Carnegie Institution of Washington, 1953), 1–198, plates 1–75.

16. Herb Meyer, "The Oligocene Lyons Flora of Northwestern Oregon," *Ore Bin* 35 (1973): 37–51.

17. Herbert W. Meyer, "An Evaluation of the Methods for Estimating Paleoaltitudes Using Tertiary Floras from the Rio Grande Rift Vicinity" (PhD diss., University of California, Berkeley, 1986), v–vii, 1–217.

18. *Partners in Paleontology: Proceedings of the Fourth Conference on Fossil Resources,* ed. Margaret Johnston and James McChristal (Denver: National Park Service, 1997), 1–239.

19. Herbert W. Meyer, *The Fossils of Florissant* (Washington, D.C.: Smithsonian Books, 2003), 1–258.

20. Explore the World of Florissant Paleontology, http://planning.nps.gov/flfo/.

21. T. D. A. Cockerell, "Colorado a Million Years Ago," *American Museum Journal* 16, no. 7 (1916): 444.

22. MacGinitie, *Fossil Plants of the Florissant Beds, Colorado,* 8.

23. April Kinchloe, "A Taxonomic and Morphometric Study of the Eocene Spiders from Florissant, Colorado" (master's thesis, University of Colorado, Boulder, 2004), 1–139.

24. Defenders of Florissant, press release, June 12, 1969, FLFO-424, Florissant Fossil Beds National Monument Archives, Colorado.

25. Karen J. Lloyd, Marie P. Worley-Georg, and Jaelyn J. Eberle, "The Chadronian Mammalian Fauna of the Florissant Formation, Florissant Fossil Beds National Monument, Colorado," in *Paleontology of the Upper Eocene Florissant Formation, Colorado: Geological Society of America Special Paper 435,* ed. Herbert W. Meyer and Dena M. Smith (Boulder, CO: Geological Society of America, 2008), 117–26.

26. National Park Service Public Use Statistics Office, "NPS Stats," www.nature.nps. gov/stats/.

27. Harry D. MacGinitie, interview by Earle Kittleman, September 21, 1979, FLFO-375, Florissant Fossil Beds National Monument Archives, Colorado.

CHAPTER SEVEN

1. David R. Collins, *Farmworker's Friend: The Story of Cesar Chavez* (Minneapolis: Carolrhoda Books, 1996).

2. Luther J. Carter, "DDT Critics Attempt to Ban Its Use in Wisconsin," *Science* 163, no. 3867 (February 7, 1969): 548–50.

3. Victor John Yannacone, jr., "The Origins of Our National Environmental Policy," in *Future Land Use: Energy, Environmental and Legal Constraints,* eds. R. W. Burchell and D. Listokin (New Brunswick, NJ: Rutgers University, 1975): 145–89.

4. William H. Rodgers Jr., "The Most Creative Moments in the History of Environmental Law: 'The Whats,'" *University of Illinois Law Review* 2000, no. 1 (2000).

5. Von Russell Creel, Bob Burke, and Kenny A. Franks, *The American Jurist: The Life of Judge Alfred P. Murrah* (Oklahoma City: Oklahoma Heritage Association, 1996), 108.

6. Creel et al., *The American Jurist,* 120.

7. Ibid., 121.

8. Ibid., 120.

9. Victor John Yannacone, jr., Bernard S. Cohen, and Steven G. Davison, *Environmental Rights and Remedies*, vol. 1 (New York: Lawyers Co-operative Pub. Co., 1972).

10. Richard Lamm, interview by John Stansfield, Spring 2008.

11. Roger Hansen to Estella B. Leopold, e-mail, April 7 and June 10, 2009.

12. "Conversation: A New Say in Court," *Time*, October 24, 1969.

13. Herbert W. Meyer, *The Fossils of Florissant* (Washington, D.C.: Smithsonian Books, 2003), 1–258.

14. *Paleontology of the Upper Eocene Florissant Formation, Colorado: Geological Society of America Special Paper 435*, ed. Herbert W. Meyer and Dena M. Smith (Boulder, CO: Geological Society of America, 2008).

15. Estella B. Leopold and Scott T. Clay-Poole, "Florissant Leaf and Pollen Floras of Colorado Compared: Climatic Implications," in *Fossil Flora and Stratigraphy of the Florissant Formation, Colorado. Proceedings of the Denver Museum of Nature & Science* 4, no. 1, ed. Emmett Evanoff, Kathryn M. Gregory-Wodzicki, and Kirk R. Johnson (Denver: Denver Museum of Nature & Science, 2001), 17–69; F. H. Wingte and D. J. Nichols, "Palynology of the Uppermost Eocene Lacustrine Deposits of Florissant Fossil Beds National Monument, Colorado," in *Fossil Flora and Stratigraphy of the Florissant Formation, Colorado*, 71–135.

16. Elisabeth A. Wheeler, "Fossil Dicotyledonous Woods from Florissant Fossil Beds National Monument, Colorado," in *Fossil Flora and Stratigraphy of the Florissant Formation, Colorado*, 187–203.

17. Aldo Leopold, *A Sand County Almanac* (New York: Oxford University Press, 1949).

18. Richard Louv, *Last Child in the Woods: Saving Our Children from Nature-Deficit Disorder* (Chapel Hill, NC: Algonquin Books, 2008), 1–336.

APPENDIX

1. William C. McIntosh and Charles E. Chapin, "Geochronology of the Central Colorado Volcanic Field," *New Mexico Bureau of Geology and Mineral Resources Bulletin* 160 (2004): 205–37.

2. Emmett Evanoff, William C. McIntosh, and Paul C. Murphey, "Stratigraphic Summary and ^{40}Ar/^{39}Ar Geochronology of the Florissant Formation, Colorado," in *Fossil Flora and Stratigraphy of the Florissant Formation, Colorado. Proceedings of the Denver Museum of Nature & Science* 4, no. 1, ed. Emmett Evanoff, Kathryn M. Gregory-Wodzicki, and Kirk R. Johnson. Denver: Denver Museum of Nature & Science, (2001), 1–16.

3. Various newspaper reports summarized in James McChristal, "A History of Florissant Fossil Beds National Monument: In Celebration of Preservation" (unpublished report, FLFO-423, Florissant Fossil Beds National Monument Archives, 1994), 1–106.

4. Jessie A. Paylor to Florissant Fossil Beds National Monument Superintendant, October 29, 1990, FLFO-166, Florissant Fossil Beds National Monument Archives, Colorado.

5. Elisabeth A. Wheeler, "Fossil Dicotyledonous Woods from Florissant Fossil Beds National Monument, Colorado," in *Fossil Flora and Stratigraphy of the Florissant Formation, Colorado*, 187–203.

6. Herbert W. Meyer, *The Fossils of Florissant* (Washington, D.C.: Smithsonian Books, 2003), 1–258.

7. Estella B. Leopold and Scott T. Clay-Poole, "Fossil Leaf and Pollen Floras of Colorado Compared: Climatic Implications," in *Fossil Flora and Stratigraphy of the Florissant Formation, Colorado*, 17–69.

8. Meyer, *The Fossils of Florissant*, 1–258.

9. Karen J. Lloyd, Marie P. Worley-Georg, and Jaelyn J. Eberle, "The Chadronian Mammalian Fauna of the Florissant Formation, Florissant Fossil Beds National Monument, Colorado," in *Paleontology of the Upper Eocene Florissant Formation, Colorado: Geological Society of America Special Paper 435*, ed. Herbert W. Meyer and Dena M. Smith (Boulder, CO: Geological Society of America, 2008), 117–26.

10. Herbert W. Meyer, "A Review of the Paleoelevation Estimates from the Florissant Flora, Colorado," in *Fossil Flora and Stratigraphy of the Florissant Formation, Colorado*, 205–16.

11. Harry D. MacGinitie, *Fossil Plants of the Florissant Beds, Colorado*, Carnegie Institution of Washington publication 599 (Washington, D.C.: Carnegie Institution of Washington, 1953), 49–54.

12. Dena M. Smith, "A Comparison of Plant-Insect Associations in the Middle Eocene Green River Formation and the Upper Eocene Florissant Formation and Their Climatic Implications," in *Paleontology of the Upper Eocene Florissant Formation, Colorado*, 89–103.

13. Thomas C. Emmel, Marc C. Minno, and Boyce A. Drummond, *Fossil Butterflies: A Guide to the Present and Fossil Species of Central Colorado* (Stanford, CA: Stanford University Press, 1992).

14. Mary Ellen Benson, "Exceptional Diversity in Late Eocene Freshwater Diatoms from the Florissant Formation, Teller County, Colorado," Abstract, *Geological Society of America Abstracts with Programs* 38, no. 7 (2006): 381.

15. *Paracarpinus* referenced in Steven R. Manchester and Peter R. Crane, "A New Genus of Betulaceae from the Oligocene of Western North America," *Botanical Gazette* 148, no. 2 (1987): 263–73. *Fagopsis* referenced in Steven R. Manchester and Peter R. Crane, "Attached Leaves, Inflorescences, and Fruits of *Fagopsis*, an Extinct Genus of Fagaceous Affinity from the Oligocene Florissant Flora of Colorado, U.S.A.," *American Journal of Botany* 70, no. 8 (1983): 1147–64. *Cedrelospermum* referenced in Steven R. Manchester, "Attached Reproductive and Vegetative Remains of the Extinct American-European Genus *Cedrelospermum* (Ulmaceae) from the Early Tertiary of Utah and Colorado," *American Journal of Botany* 76, no. 2 (1989): 256–76.

Suggested Reading

Brues, Charles T. "Fossil Parasitic and Phytophagous Hymenoptera from Florissant, Colorado." *Bulletin of the American Museum of Natural History* 22 (1906): 491–98.

Cockerell, T. D. A. "Colorado a Million Years Ago." *American Museum Journal* 16, no. 7 (1916): 442–50.

———. "Florissant: A Miocene Pompeii." *Popular Science Monthly* 74 (1908): 112–26.

———. "Some Old-World Types of Insects in the Miocene of Colorado." *Science* 26 (1907): 446–47.

Cook, Terri, and Lon Abbott. "Florissant Fossil Beds: An Eocene Time Capsule." *Earth* (July 2011): 48–52.

Creel, Von Russell, Bob Burke, and Kenny A. Franks. *The American Jurist: The Life of Judge Alfred P. Murrah*. Oklahoma City: Oklahoma Heritage Association, 1996.

Epis, Rudy C. "Proposed Florissant Fossil Beds National Monument." *Mines Magazine* 59 (1969): 10–13.

Evanoff, Emmett, Kathryn M. Gregory-Wodzicki, and Kirk R. Johnson, eds. *Fossil Flora and Stratigraphy of the Florissant Formation, Colorado. Proceedings of the Denver Museum of Nature & Science* 4, no. 1. Denver: Denver Museum of Nature & Science, 2001.

Gamer, Eleanor E. "The Fossil Beds of Florissant." *National Parks Magazine* (July 1965): 16–19.

Jacobsen, Stephen R., and Douglas J. Nichols. "Florissant: An Ancient Flora Preserved." *Garden* (March/April 1981): 19–23.

Leopold, Estella B. "Housing Subdivisions vs. Florissant Fossils." *Trail & Timberline* 573 (September 1966).

Leopold, Estella B., and Scott T. Clay-Poole. "Florissant Leaf and Pollen Floras of Colorado Compared: Climatic Implications." In *Fossil Flora and Stratigraphy of the Florissant Formation, Colorado. Proceedings of the Denver Museum of Nature & Science* 4, no. 1. Edited by Emmett Evanoff, Kathryn M. Gregory-Wodzicki, and Kirk R. Johnson, 17–69. Denver: Denver Museum of Nature & Science, 2001.

Leopold, Estella B., and Harry D. MacGinitie. "Development and Affinities of Tertiary Floras in the Rocky Mountains." In *Floristics and Paleofloristics of Asia and Eastern North America*. Edited by A. Graham, 147–200. Amsterdam: Elsevier, 1972.

Lesquereux, Leo. *Contributions to the Fossil Flora of the Western Territories. Part III: The Cretaceous and Tertiary Floras. United States Geological Survey of the Territories Report* 8 (1883): 1–283, 60 plates.

MacGinitie, Harry D. *Fossil Plants of the Florissant Beds, Colorado.* Carnegie Institution of Washington publication 599. Washington, D.C.: Carnegie Institute of Washington, 1953.

Manchester, Steven R., and Peter R. Crane. "Attached Leaves, Inflorescences, and Fruits of *Fagopsis*, an Extinct Genus of Fagaceous Affinity from the Oligocene Florissant Flora of Colorado, U.S.A." *American Journal of Botany* 70 (1983): 1147–64.

Melander, Axel Leonard. "A Report on Some Miocene Diptera from Florissant, Colorado." *American Museum Novitates* 1407 (1949): 1–63.

Meyer, Herbert W. *The Fossils of Florissant.* Washington, D.C.: Smithsonian Institution Press, 2003.

Meyer, Herbert W., and Dena M. Smith, eds. *Paleontology of the Upper Eocene Florissant Formation, Colorado: Geological Society of America Special Paper 435.* Boulder, CO: Geological Society of America, 2008.

Meyer, Herbert W., Steven W. Veatch, and Amanda Cook. "Field Guide to the Paleontology and Volcanic Setting of the Florissant Fossil Beds, Colorado." In *Field Trips in the Southern Rocky Mountains, USA.* Edited by E. P. Nelson and E. A. Erslev, 151–66. Boulder, CO: Geological Society of America Publications, 2004.

Meyer, Herbert W., and Laine Weber. "Florissant Fossil Beds National Monument Preservation of an Ancient Ecosystem." *Rocks and Minerals* 70 (July/August 1995): 232–39.

Nudds, John R., and Paul A. Selden. "Florissant." In *Fossil Ecosystems of North America: A Guide to the Sites and Their Extraordinary Biotas,* 205–32. London: Manson Publishing, 2008.

Roueché, Berton. "A Reporter at Large: A Window on the Oligocene." The *New Yorker,* November 13, 1971.

Scudder, Samuel Hubbard. *Adephagous and Clavicorn Coleoptera from the Tertiary Deposits at Florissant, Colorado, with Descriptions of a Few other Forms and a Systematic List of the Non-Rhynchophorous Tertiary Coleoptera of North America. Monographs of the United States Geological Survey* 40 (1900): 1–148, 11 plates.

———. *The Tertiary Insects of North America. United States Geological Survey of the Territories Report* 13 (1890): 1–734, 28 plates.

———. *Tertiary Rhynchophorus Coleoptera of the United States. Monographs of the United States Geological Survey* 21 (1893): 1–206, 12 plates.

U.S. Congress. *A Bill to Provide for the Establishment of the Florissant Fossil Beds National Monument in the State of Colorado: Hearing on S. 912, Before the Committee on Interior and Insular Affairs Subcommittee on Parks and Recreation.* 91st Cong., 1st Sess. (May 29, 1969).

Wickham, H. F. "New Miocene Coleoptera from Florissant." *Bulletin of the Museum of Comparative Zoology at Harvard College* 58 (1914): 423–94, 16 plates.

Yannacone, Victor John, jr., Bernard S. Cohen, and Steven G. Davison. *Environmental Rights and Remedies,* 2 vols. New York: Lawyers Co-operative Pub. Co., 1972.

Dramatis Personae

ROGER P. HANSEN was co-founder and CEO of the Colorado Open Space Coordinating Council (now the Colorado Environmental Coalition). Later he served as CEO of the Rocky Mountain Center on Environment, which he also founded. He taught environmental law at the University of Denver, Colorado School of Mines, and Pacific Lutheran University for a number of years before retiring to the Puget Sound region. He later returned to Denver, where he taught part time at the University of Denver Law School. Roger is now retired and living in Aurora, Colorado.

RICHARD LAMM served in the Colorado legislature for eight years and then for twelve years as governor of Colorado from 1975 to 1987. As a first-year legislator, he drafted and championed passage of the nation's first liberalized abortion law. He was an early leader of the environmental movement, and was president of the first national Conference on Population and the Environment. He worked closely with the Colorado Mountain Club and served as its first conservation chair. Lamm is a prolific writer on a wide range of subjects, including population growth, immigration, health care reform, and the politics of Colorado. He currently teaches at the University of Denver, where he is director of the Center for Public Policy and Contemporary Issues.

TOM LAMM established his law practice, Butler and Lamm, in 1969 in Boulder, Colorado, after serving as clerk for Senior Judge Orie L. Phillips of the Tenth Circuit Court of Appeals in Denver, Colorado. His legal cases have been diverse, involving environmental law, commercial litigation, criminal defense, personal injury, and other matters. His civil trial work has resulted in numerous multimillion-dollar verdicts and settlements. Lamm is a former member of the Colorado Supreme Court Grievance Committee Hearing Board and former chairman of the Just Care, Inc., health care organization, among other appointments. Butler and Lamm is now located in Louisville, Colorado.

ESTELLA B. LEOPOLD held a career position as research scientist in paleobotany for the U.S. Geological Survey in Denver, carrying out field and laboratory work from 1956 to 1975. In 1971, she was visiting professor in environmental studies at the University of Wisconsin. Leopold then moved to Seattle in 1975 to become director of the Quaternary Research Center of the University of Washington, and taught as professor in the Department of Botany there until her retirement in 2000. She has published about one hundred scientific articles, mainly focusing on the geological history of forests and prairie in the western United States. She was elected to the National Academy of Science and the American Philosophical Society. She is the recipient of the International Cosmos Prize for 2010 offered by the Japanese Expo '90 Foundation for her work in conservation.

HARRY D. MACGINITIE remained active as a research associate at the University of California Museum of Paleontology following his retirement from a long career of teaching at Humboldt State College. He was an inspiration to many budding paleobotanists, including authors Leopold and Meyer. Besides his authoritative Florissant monograph, he published monographs on six other important fossil floras of the western United States. He passed away in 1987.

HERBERT W. MEYER has been the paleontologist at Florissant Fossil Beds National Monument since 1994. He is the author of *The Fossils of Florissant* (2003) and a number of other publications dealing with modern views of the Florissant flora. He is adjunct faculty at the University of Colorado at Boulder and has served on various committees for graduate students who have done research at Florissant. He completed his doctorate in paleontology at the University of California at Berkeley in 1986.

BEATRICE (BETTIE) WILLARD became an internationally recognized alpine ecologist. She served as head of the Seminar on Environmental Arts and Sciences conferences for the Thorne Ecological Institute in Boulder, Colorado. Her experience with the conferences and knowledge of industry and ecology led to her appointment by President Richard Nixon to the Council of Environmental Quality in 1972, where she was the first ecologist and the first woman appointee and served for nearly five years. Bettie worked tirelessly while in Washington, D.C., on projects such as the Trans-Alaska Pipeline, to ensure environmental protection during development. Returning to Boulder, Bettie was involved in writing and speaking engagements. Her books include *Land Above the Trees* with Ann Zwinger (1972), *Alpine Wildflowers* with Michael Smithson (1980), *A Roadside Guide to Rocky Mountain National Park* with Susan Foster (1990), and *Plants of Rocky Mountain National Park* with Linda Beidleman and Richard Beidleman (2000). She passed away in 2003.

Toward the end of 1969, Estella Leopold and Bettie Willard received State Conservationist of the Year awards from the Colorado Wildlife Federation, in cooperation with the National Wildlife Federation and the Sears Roebuck Foundation. The award plaques bore two handsome bald eagle statues with brass plates, which read, "for outstanding contributions to the wise use and management of the nation's natural resources."

VIM CRANE WRIGHT, after following the Florissant developments in the press, swung into action collecting funds for the court cases in 1969. She served as president and founder of the Denver Audubon Society (now Audubon Society of Greater Denver) and was a two-term president of the Colorado Open Space Council (1970–1972). Vim served as assistant director of the Institute for Environmental Studies at the University of Washington from 1976 to her retirement in 1995. She was the recipient of the first Feinstone Environmental Award (1976) from the State University of New York College of Environmental Science and Forestry. Wright was the founder and co-founder of several important environmental groups in Washington State. She served as chair of the Citizen Group Members of the Institute of Ecology, a nonprofit group based in Washington, D.C., from 1973 to 1982. She passed away in 2003.

VICTOR JOHN YANNACONE, JR., is a pioneer in environmental litigation. He still maintains an active legal career and has written extensively on environmental law and a number of other legal issues. He coauthored a significant and frequently quoted two-volume treatise, *Environmental Rights and Remedies*, in 1972, and has published a number of law articles. He has lectured widely on environment, the law, and a number of public policy issues, including science education, energy policy, land use, and resource management. His work to limit the use of persistent pesticides, particularly DDT, has produced benefits for natural environments throughout the world. Together with his wife, Carol Yannacone, he was a co-founder of the Environmental Defense Fund and served as its attorney in their early legal successes, culminating in preventing completion of the poorly considered Cross-Florida Barge Canal and the Everglades Jetport. He is the founder of the Environmental Law Section of the American Trial Lawyers Association. He still practices at the law firm he founded with his father in 1960, Yannacone & Yannacone, of Patchogue, New York. Victor was a regular member of the Geological Society of America for many years and an associate member of the American Association of Petroleum Geologists.

Index

Page numbers in italics indicate illustrations.